FAST FACTS™ ON MORMONISM

John Ankerberg
& John Weldon

HARVEST HOUSE™ PUBLISHERS
EUGENE, OREGON

Cover by Terry Dugan Design, Minneapolis, Minnesota

FAST FACTS™ ON MORMONISM

Published by Harvest House Publishers
Eugene, Oregon 97402

Library of Congress Cataloging-in-Publication Data

Ankerberg, John, 1945-
Fast facts on Mormonism / John Ankerberg, John Weldon.
p. cm.
Includes bibliographical references.
ISBN 0-7369-1079-4 (pbk.)
1. Mormon Church—Controversial literature. I. Weldon, John. II. Title.
BX8645 .A684 2003
289.3—dc21 2002014463

Printed in the United States of America

03 04 05 06 07 08 09 / BC-MS / 10 9 8 7 6 5 4 3 2 1

Contents

Authors' Note

This book is part of a series of short "Fast Facts" books designed to help the reader understand the basic facts that support the claims and the truth of Christianity. Some books in the series will deal with the evidence directly and some with evaluating the claims of other faiths or movements. Some readers may want to explore some of the questions posed in more detail.

For deeper study, the reader is encouraged to seek out many of the fine books listed in the extensive notes section at the end of this book, especially the following:

Jerald and Sandra Tanner, *The Changing World of Mormonism.*

Bill McKeever, Eric Johnson, *Mormonism 101: Examining the Religion of the Latter-day Saints.*

Bob Witte, *Where Does it Say That?* (www.irr.org).

Institute for Religious Research, *The Book of Mormon Today* (www.irr.org).

D. Michael Quinn, *Early Mormonism and the Magic World View* (2nd Edition).

David Persuitte, *Joseph Smith and the Origins of the Book of Mormon* (2nd Edition).

Smith Research Associates, *New Mormon Studies CD-ROM: A Comprehensive Resource Library.*

Brent Lee Metcalfe (Editor), *New Approaches to the Book of Mormon: Explorations in Critical Methodology.*

Richard N. Ostling, Joan K. Ostling, *Mormon America: The Power and the Promise.*

Francis J. Beckwith, Carl Mosser and Paul Owen, eds., *The New Mormon Challenge: Responding to the Latest Defenses of a Fast-Growing Movement.*

Kenneth D. Boa, Robert M. Bowman, Jr., *Faith Has Its Reasons: An Integrative Approach to Defending Christianity.*

Websites

Utah Lighthouse Ministry (www.utlm.org)

Recovery from Mormonism (exmormon.org)

Tapestry Against Polygamy (polygamy.org)

Alpha & Omega Ministries (aomin.org)

Institute for Religious Research (irr.org)

Child Protection Project (LDS abuse information) (childpro.org)

Close Look at Mormonism (www.mindspring.com/~engineer_my_dna/mormon/).

MormonAlliance (abuse information) (mormonalliance.org).

Mormonism Research Ministry (mrm.org).

Reason - Dedicated to Filling In the Missing Pieces of the Mormon History Puzzle (http://www.xmission.com/~country/reason/reason.htm). (See "A One-page Course in Mormonism" and the links section on that page.)

Alpha Ministries (www.alphamin.org).

This list was revised and updated from *The Encyclopedia of Cults and New Religions.*

"We are Christians in a very real sense and that is coming to be more and more widely recognized. Once upon a time people everywhere said we are not Christians. They have come to recognize that we are, and that we have a very vital and dynamic religion based on the teachings of Jesus Christ."[1]

—LDS President Gordon B. Hinckley

SECTION I
INTRODUCTION

1

WHY IS MORMONISM IMPORTANT?

For the first time ever, the Church of Jesus Christ of Latter-day Saints (LDS) is now the fifth-largest religious faith in America. It will shortly replace the Church of God as the fourth largest religious body in America.[1] It has a global Church membership of 12 million people in 160 nations. Indeed, there are now more Mormons than Evangelical Lutherans, Presbyterians, or Episcopalians. According to the *Deseret News Church Almanac*, of its nearly 300,000 yearly converts, up to 80 percent are drawn from Protestant backgrounds, meaning that millions of people have abandoned their Christian heritage in favor of Mormonism.

Mormonism is broadly appealing for several reasons, including its emphasis on moral values and its stress upon maintaining strong family relationships. In addition, it offers numerous social benefits to members. In many ways it is by far the most successful among the thousands of new religions founded in the last 200 years.

The need for *Fast Facts on Mormonism* arises from specific claims made by the Mormon church that have caused widespread confusion concerning the precise nature of Mormonism. For instance, Mormonism claims to represent true Christianity and to believe in the biblical God. It teaches that it trusts in the true Jesus Christ and that He alone is the atoning Savior who died for the sins of the world. Indeed, a recent Barna poll revealed the following surprising information: "In total, 34% of the adults who attend a Mormon church say they have made a personal commitment to Christ that is important in their life today and also say that when they die they know they will go to Heaven solely because they have confessed their sins and accepted Jesus Christ as their savior."[2]

But is Mormonism truly Christian as is increasingly argued? We hope to clear up this confusion on two fronts. First, we will show that even though Mormon literature frequently uses biblical and Christian terms, they are given entirely different meanings. If the meanings are radically different, it is unlikely that the message is going to be the same. Second, we hope to inform Mormons themselves, who are often unaware of important features of LDS faith, through a sampling of their religion's factual history and teachings.

The reason for the current confusion stems from the similarity of terminology and the fact that in recent years the LDS church has initiated a powerful campaign to influence millions of people with its message that it is truly Christian. Sophisticated magazine, newspaper, and television ads have reached tens of millions of people with the claims of Mormonism. Multiple full-page newspaper inserts proclaim, "We believe the New Testament Scriptures are true and that they testify that Jesus is indeed the Promised Messiah and Savior of the world." Headlines read, "Mormons believe Jesus Christ is Lord and Savior" and "Mormons testify Jesus is the Christ." These advertisements, also placed in *Reader's Digest* and *TV Guide*, include an 800 number that respondents can call to receive a free copy of the Bible *and* the *Book of Mormon*, which is boldly advertised as "another testament of Jesus Christ."

The success of these ads is evident. In 1989, almost 260,000 requests for a free *Book of Mormon* were received, and 86,000 of those responding wanted missionaries to make a personal visit. In addition, 40 percent of the respondents said they "believed the book was the Word of God" and that "they had a special feeling about it."[3] (Some 109 million copies of the *Book of Mormon* have been published since 1830, according to the official LDS website.) By the late 1990s, these television campaigns sometimes ran twice during a one-hour program and had continuing positive responses.

In the new millennium, LDS efforts at conversion have intensified and continue to bear fruit, as evidenced by 300,000 new converts per year. Indeed, some 40 percent of the population of the United States has now been personally visited by representatives of the Mormon Church.[4]

Half a Billion Mormons?

The rapid rise in converts is one reason Mormonism should be taken seriously by the evangelical community. Recent dramatic growth projections may be legitimate. According to *The New Mormon Challenge:* "If one recalculates from 1997 membership figures with the same rate of growth [Rodney] Stark used in his initial [1984] study, Mormonism will have a membership of over 580 million by the end of the twentieth century." Whether or not these projections are valid, Mormonism will continue to have significant growth rates. Further, the 65–70,000 LDS missionaries "make the LDS church the single largest missionary-sending organization in the world." Also, "within the next 50 years the LDS church could easily have a full-time missionary force of 400,000 converting more than 2.5 million people annually… [and] be larger than all Protestant and Catholic missionary efforts combined."[5]

Of even greater concern, "almost all converts to Mormonism come from a nominal Christian background." Although no scientific studies yet exist, "according to several 'eyeball' estimates I have seen or heard reported, 75–80 percent of Mormon converts come from specifically Protestant backgrounds" and "…far more people convert to Mormonism from evangelical churches than vice versa." "Thus, Mormon growth largely depends on the prior success of Protestant and Catholic missionaries. This provides a third important reason why evangelicals cannot afford to shrug off predictions of Mormon growth: Mormon missionaries don't evangelize, they proselytize. Mormonism is a religion that gets its life mostly from preexisting forms of Christianity. The predictions of incredible growth for the LDS church are also predictions of loss for Protestant, Catholic, and, to a lesser extent, Orthodox Churches—with Protestantism sustaining the greatest losses (though that could easily change)."[6]

In conclusion, Mormonism is a topic the Christian church cannot afford to ignore. The large majority of Mormons are former Christians, nominal or not. It is ironic that the LDS church owes its great success to the previous efforts of dedicated Christian workers who painstakingly "plowed the field," so that LDS missionaries could "pick the fruit."

If the current LDS membership of 12 million is expected to double in the next 10 years, is there a Christian anywhere who can be unconcerned?

2

HOW INFLUENTIAL IS MORMONISM?

Direct advertising is not the only way the Mormon church seeks converts. Its methods of proselytizing are as varied as its corporate holdings. For example, the church takes advantage of the fact that every year six to seven million people visit an island paradise:

> Mormons own a substantial portion of Hawaii [including] the major financial institutions of this area. When you go to the [Mormon sponsored] Polynesian Culture Center they offer you a tour to [visit] their Temple....Soon after you return from your visit...you will receive a knock from a Mormon missionary asking how you enjoyed your visit and whether you would like to know more about the

> Church. The Mormons have many other ways of recruiting members: through door-to-door missionaries, visitor centers, the thousands of church-sponsored Boy Scout troops and educational institutions, and...the Marriott Hotel chain which places Mormon literature in every room.[7]

Moreover, the church maintains financial assets valued in the tens of billions of dollars, a testimony to the power of faithful tithing by members. In the U.S., tithing brings in an estimated $1 billion per year, and about $5 to $6 billion globally. (Members who tithe are even promised escape from divine judgment: "Behold, now it is called today until the coming of the Son of Man, and verily it is a day of sacrifice, and a day for the tithing of my people; for he that is tithed shall not be burned at his coming" (*Doctrine and Covenants* [*D&C*] 64:23). In 1991, *Time* magazine reported, "In business terms, the Church is an $8 billion-a-year conglomerate that employs about 10,000 people."[8] In 1999, Richard N. and Joan K. Ostling, wrote in *Mormon America* that the church has an "estimated $25 to $30 billion in assets."[9]

Mormonism is one of the wealthiest churches per capita on earth. Not unexpectedly, many of the lay leaders within the Mormon church are businessmen who help the church oversee its vast and growing worldwide financial empire. For example, the church owns real-estate management and trust-holding firms that alone have assets of several billion dollars. In addition, it owns or has owned a half-dozen insurance companies, 2 newspapers, 2 television stations, a chain of bookstores, a shopping mall, 16 radio stations, hundreds of thousands of acres of farmland, one of the nation's largest private television networks and most of Salt Lake City's tallest skyscrapers.[10]

The church is also a large stockholder in Utah Power and Light Company, with assets of more than one billion dollars. The Mormon empire runs several large international corporations like PepsiCo and the Marriott Corporation, several colleges, such as Brigham Young University (with 60 language departments and an enrollment of more than 30,000 students), plus other schools, factories, and businesses. According to the late Dr. Walter Martin, the church owns Bonneville International Corporation, Zion's Securities Corporation, Deseret Ranches of Florida, and some 315,000 acres near Disney World, which are worth at least a billion dollars.[11] According to *The God Makers*, a critical film on Mormonism, "the Mormon Church is the second largest financial institution west of the Mississippi River. They own the $2.6 million Beneficial Life Insurance Company, The Deseret Management and Trust Corp., hospitals, schools, apartment buildings, and farms. They are a major stockholder in the *LA Times*. They own TV and radio stations (and) the ZCMI Department Store chain. They have vast land holdings with ownerships in all 50 American states, throughout Canada and Europe and on every continent. Two thirds of their properties are tax exempt."[12] In 2002, Salt Lake City's only independent paper, the *Salt Lake Tribune*, was taken over by the LDS church in what appears to have been a hostile capture.[13]

Mormons tend to view financial prosperity as a sign of God's blessing (see Alma 1:29; 4 Nephi 1:23). Their corporate wealth confirms their belief that Mormonism is wealthy because it is pleasing to God. Again, tithing is a principal means of church income. According to Mormon doctrine, tithing is a law of God commanded upon the people. *Doctrine and Covenants* 119:3-4 calls it a "standing law...forever." A former devoted church member estimates that many Mormons "will be paying 20% to 25% of their gross income to the Church."[14] Wealthy Mormon celebrities and business executives also tend to tithe generously. For example, the Osmond and Marriott families are two large contributors to the Mormon empire.[15]

In state and national politics, Mormons have gained more than their share of influence. Richard Beal, one of the most powerful men in the Reagan administration, was a Mormon.[16] Mormons have held the following posts and headed the following departments: Assistant Attorney General, head of the National Security Council, Secretary of Agriculture, Treasurer of the United States, the United States Department of Commerce, the Department of Interior, the Federal Communications Commission, the Department of Housing and Urban Development, the Federal Research Board, the Securities and Exchange Commission, and various state government posts.[17] Mormons also head or have headed Walt Disney Productions, Sav-On Drugs, Max Factor, Standard Oil, and many other conglomerates.[18]

The Mormon church is the single largest sponsor of Boy Scout units in the United States (17,000), and Mormon officials have admitted this is an effective manner in which to share the faith.[19] Former Secretary of Agriculture in the Eisenhower administration and the former Mormon prophet and president, Ezra Taft Benson, commented: "Scouting is Church work. It is part of the [Mormon] Church program.[20] He also said,

> I have been deeply impressed with the record that has been made by the Church....In no other field do we have a better reputation than in the field of Scouting....We have...a higher proportion of Scout troops sponsored by the Church than any other church or civic organization in the world.... [And] we have the highest enrollment of boys in Scouting of any church on the earth.[21]
>
> Religious emphasis is a part of Scouting....Scouting helps prepare boys for [Mormon] Church responsibility....We want these boys to become better men and boys and honor their [Mormon] priesthood and to be faithful members of the [Mormon] Church and kingdom of God.[22]

In essence, the power and positive image of Mormonism is undergirded by many factors—their financial reputation, their scouting leadership, their moral emphasis, and their Christian appearance. All this is why many Christians believe the Mormon church is a Christian organization and that Mormons are Christians.

As mentioned earlier, the Mormon church's successful portrayal of itself as Christian explains why there are apparently more converts to Mormonism from Christian churches than there are official defections from Mormonism. As one Mormon magazine noted: "Far more persons convert to the Mormon Church from other churches or from a status of no religious affiliation than leave."[23] The report cited a 1990 study published by Mormons Howard M. Bahr and David Hunt relying on the National Opinion Research Center's (NORC) General Social Survey data, 1972–1988, and the University of Wisconsin National Survey of Families and Households, 1987–1988. This study also indicated that the conversion rates from various Christian denominations to Mormonism were proportionately similar. However, Jewish, Catholic, Baptist, and Christian Reformed churches had somewhat lower conversion rates than several evangelical and fundamentalist denominations and some mainline denominations (Presbyterian, Episcopal, Christian, and United Churches of Christ, among others). Studies also indicated that among leading world religions, Mormonism has the fourth highest retention rate: Islam (92 percent), Jewish (88 percent), Catholic (83.5 percent), Mormon (82 percent).[24] But such studies do not give us the whole picture. For example, according to the *Los Angeles Times*, several analysts familiar with the Mormon church have stated that some 40 percent of Mormons are inactive and that many of these are disillusioned.[25] But if even 30 percent of Mormons are inactive or disillusioned, the Mormon empire could face some serious future problems.

Influencing Christians?

Christians need to know that the LDS church has programs specifically designed to reach and convert them to Mormonism. There are courses that teach LDS church leaders to befriend and reach Christian clergy. In one seminar, "Win a Minister and Influence a Thousand," attendees were encouraged to influence pastors to reach their flocks with the message of Mormonism. Daryl Anderson's "Love Thy Minister Neighbor Workshop Outline" has 39 suggestions for reaching Christian ministers. Programs like these have had success among liberal and mainline denominations. Indeed, there are many Mormons who promote their religion strategically through several popular plans and courses. One example is the multimillion-dollar bestseller by Stephen Covey, *The 7 Habits of Highly Effective People* (millions have attended courses based on this book).

> These individuals are committed Mormons whose venues have had a large impact in Christian circles: [Covey's] book *The Divine Center* (1982) is about centering one's life in the god of Mormonism and reads like an LDS primer. In fact, it seems to be the basis for *SH [Seven Habits]* as many of the ideas Covey wrote in it in 1982 are included and built upon in the *SH*, published in 1989....Covey's organization, the Franklin Covey Company, claims to have over 19,000 licensed client facilitators teaching its curriculum to over 750,000 participants annually. Yearly book sales are more than 1.5 million with over 15 million individuals using their planner products. Included among these participants and book purchasers are Christians, including business leaders, pastors and denominational leaders.[26]

Bill Gordon, with the Southern Baptist Convention's North America Mission Board, points out that

> many church and religious organizations are using this program to train ministers and leaders. One of the reasons they find this program attractive is because it gives a prominent place to spirituality in personal growth. However, most of those who take this training are unaware of the specific religious beliefs that are behind many of Covey's principles. Covey has stated these religious beliefs in an earlier book entitled *The Divine Center.* This book contains many of the same principles that are found in *7 Habits.* Many of the anecdotes and illustrations in the two books are also similar. An analysis of *The Divine Center* reveals that Covey's religious beliefs are Mormon. Covey explains in this book that he has discovered how to communicate Mormon truths to non-Mormons by simply changing his vocabulary. He writes, "I have found in

> speaking to various non-LDS groups in different cultures that we can teach and testify of many gospel [LDS] principles if we are careful in selecting words which carry our meaning but come from their experience and frame of mind."[27]

The power and influence of Mormonism, even among evangelical Christians, is something that the Christian church needs to notice and address more thoroughly.

3

HOW DID MORMONISM BEGIN, AND WHO WAS JOSEPH SMITH?

How did Mormonism begin? The official version is recorded in the Mormon scripture *The Pearl of Great Price* (1851). By this account, the seeds of Mormonism were sown in Joseph Smith, Mormonism's founder, during a powerful divine visitation. This encounter is known as the "first vision." Allegedly, God the Father and Jesus Christ appeared to Smith as part of their plan to begin the Mormon religion and reestablish "true Christianity." As we will see later, this "first vision" episode is critical to the claims of the Mormon religion.

Joseph Smith claimed that in his fifteenth year (1820), while he was living in Manchester, New York, a religious revival of significant proportions took place and "great multitudes united themselves to the different religious parties."[28] However, Smith alleges that the doctrinal strife among these religious parties was so great as to confuse a person entirely: With such conflicting claims, how could anyone determine which religion was correct—Presbyterians, Methodists, Baptists, or any other denomination? Furthermore, according to Smith, the teachers of the various denominations allegedly "understood the same passage of Scripture so differently as to destroy all confidence in settling the question [of which group to join] by an appeal to the Bible." Because of his confusion, Smith determined to seek God's counsel as to which of the various denominations was true so that he might know which church he should join. As he explains it, James 1:5, which refers to asking God for wisdom, had a crucial impact at this juncture. In Smith's own words,

> Never did any passage of Scripture come with more power to the heart of man than this did at this time to mine. It seemed to enter with great force into every feeling of my heart. I reflected on it again and again, knowing that if any person needed wisdom from God, I did; for how to act I did not know and unless I could get more wisdom than I then had, I would never know.[29]

Smith concluded that either he must "remain in darkness and confusion" or "do as James directs, that is, ask of God."[30] In his attempt to seek God, the teenaged Joseph Smith retired to a secluded place in the woods in order to pray. He notes that it was on the morning of a "beautiful, clear day, early in the spring of 1820."[31] After finding an appropriate spot, Smith reports that he "kneeled down and began to offer up the desires of my heart to God." But what Smith encountered terrified him:

> I had scarcely done so, when immediately I was seized upon by some power which entirely overcame me, and had such an astonishing influence over me as to bind my tongue so that I could not speak. Thick darkness gathered around me, and it seemed to me for a time as if I were doomed to sudden destruction.[32]

Smith then describes how, fearing immediate death, he called upon God for deliverance:

> But, exerting all my powers to call upon God to deliver me out of the power of this enemy which had seized upon me, and at the very moment which I was ready to sink into despair and abandon myself to destruction—not to an imaginary ruin, but to the power of some actual being from the unseen world, who had such marvelous power as

> I had never before felt in any being—just at this moment of great alarm, I saw a pillar of light exactly over my head, above the brightness of the sun, which descended gradually until it fell upon me.[33]

Having felt the panic of imminent destruction, Smith was amazed to find himself delivered:

> It no sooner appeared when I found myself delivered from the enemy which held me bound. When the light rested upon me I saw two personages, whose brightness and glory defy all description, standing above me in the air. One of them spake unto me, calling me by name, and said—pointing to the other—"THIS IS MY BELOVED SON, HEAR HIM."[34]

At this point, the claims of Joseph Smith are clear. Having called on God for help, he has been immediately delivered by nothing less than the astonishing appearance of God the Father and His Son, Jesus Christ. At this juncture, Smith collected his senses and recalled his mission:

> My object in going to inquire of the Lord was to know which of all the sects was right, that I might know which to join. No sooner, therefore, did I get possession of myself, so as to be able to speak, than I asked the personages who stood above me in the light, which of all the sects was right—and which I should join.[35]

Smith was answered immediately. In fact, to answer the question of "How did Mormonism begin?" we only need read the reply that the two supernatural personages supplied to Joseph Smith's question:

> I must join none of them, for they were all wrong, and the Personage who addressed me [God the Father] said that all their creeds were an abomination in his sight: that those professors [of Christian religion] were all corrupt; that "they draw near to me with their lips, but their hearts are far from me, they teach for doctrines the commandments

> of men, having a form of godliness, but they deny the power thereof."
>
> He [God the Father] again forbade me to join with any of them; and many other things did he say unto me, which I cannot write at this time. When I came to myself again [fully regained his senses], I found myself lying on my back, looking up into heaven. When the light had departed, I had no strength; but soon recovering it in some degree, I went home.[36]

Joseph Smith had found his answer. He was convinced that God Himself had appeared to him to inform him that Christianity was an abominable, false religion. He recalls, "My mind [was] satisfied so far as the sectarian [Christian] world was concerned....[It] was not my duty to join with any of them, but to continue as I was until further directed."[37] Smith became persuaded that, out of all the men in the world, he had been uniquely called of God. Although he admits that he "frequently fell into many foolish errors," he waited patiently until the next revelation.[38]

Three years later, on September 21, 1823, Smith experienced the first of several major necromantic encounters (contacts with the dead). A spirit appeared to Smith to tell him the location of certain "gold plates." These gold plates contained the purported historical records of the Jewish "Nephite" peoples concerning their early migration to the Americas. In his *History of the Church*, Smith records the visit by this spirit, which identified itself as "Moroni" (the son of a "Nephite" historian named Mormon, the alleged author of the "gold plates" from which the *Book of Mormon* was "translated"):

> While I was thus in the act of calling upon God, I discovered a light appearing in my room, which continued to increase until the room was lighter than at noonday, when immediately a [spirit] personage appeared at my bed side, standing in the air....He called me by name, and said unto me that he was a messenger sent from the presence of God to me and that his name was Moroni; that God had a work

> for me to do....He said there was a book deposited, written upon gold plates, giving an account of the former inhabitants of this [American] continent, and the sources from whence they sprang. He also said that the fullness of the everlasting Gospel was contained in it, as delivered by the Savior [Jesus] to the ancient inhabitants [of America]; also that there were two stones in silver bows—and these stones, fastened to a breastplate, constituted what is called the Urim and Thummim—deposited with the plates; and the possession and use of these stones were what constituted [the category of] "seers" in ancient or former times; and that God had prepared them for the purpose of translating the book.[39]

In addition, the spirit quoted numerous passages of prophetic scripture, either implying or stating that some of them were about to be fulfilled. The spirit then departed, although it soon reappeared twice to state the same message.[40] Further supernatural encounters continued to influence the young Joseph Smith profoundly. The next day, the 17-year-old lad was crossing a field when suddenly his strength entirely failed him: "I fell helpless on the ground, and for a time was unconscious of anything."[41] The first thing Smith remembered was hearing the same spirit calling his name. Regaining his senses, he was commanded to go and locate the "gold plates" buried in a certain hill named Cumorah. After that, according to the spirit, he was to return yearly to that same spot for further instructions and teaching, and in the fourth year (in 1827) the translation of the "gold plates" would be permitted. These and other necromantic contacts were likely the result of Joseph Smith's use of various occult practices and magic ritual to invoke the spirit world. The specific nature of the encounters frequently fit the pattern for magical occult contacts.

By 1829, the translation was completed, and in 1830 the *Book of Mormon* was published. Named after its author, the alleged Nephite historian Mormon, it became one of the three scriptures unique to the Mormon faith (the other two are *Doctrine and Covenants* and *The Pearl of Great Price*).

By any accounting, this is quite a story. Did it really happen? Is the evidence convincing enough to warrant faith? The LDS church agrees that it stands or falls on the credibility of the first vision account. Only if it was actually God speaking to Smith is the claim of the church valid. The fact that there are more than half a dozen conflicting accounts of this "first vision" episode with major discrepancies raises suspicions. There are differences in the age of Smith, the number of divine personages (the Father and the Son, Jesus alone, "spirits" only), in the message given, and other features (for example, the reason for seeking the Lord, the manifestation of an evil presence). Jerald and Sandra Tanner's *The Case Against Mormonism* provides details that show that the first vision account as found in *The Pearl of Great Price* (1851) is not credible as the original vision of Smith, but is actually a later emended version of that experience.[42] We tend to believe Smith did see something, but that the story was embellished over time by Smith or church leaders. But assuming this really was a supernatural revelation, then the LDS scriptures could be independently tested and evaluated from many vantage points to ascertain whether they meet the criteria of divine revelation—such as consistency with previous revelation, genuine prophecy, historical accuracy, and so on.

Even though Mormon prophets and leaders have always stressed the divine authority of the *Book of Mormon*, and therefore maintained that it could withstand any and all critical scrutiny, many theologians and scholars over the years have conclusively shown the falsity of the claim from data in many disciplines. Here we will briefly highlight several of the many facts that disqualify the *Book of Mormon* from any serious consideration as true revelation from God. A full discussion can be found in our books *Behind the Mask of Mormonism* and *What Do Mormons Really Believe?* as well as the sources listed in the "Authors' Note" at the front of this book.

SECTION II

THE BOOK OF MORMON

Joseph Smith stated that "one of the grand fundamental principles of 'Mormonism' is to receive truth, let it come from whence it may."[1] Mormon Apostle Orson Pratt put it this way:

> Convince us of our errors of doctrine, if we have any, by reason, by logical arguments, or by the Word of God, and we will be ever grateful for the information, and you will ever have the pleasing reflection that you have been the instruments in the hands of God of redeeming your fellow beings from the darkness which you may see enveloping their minds. Come, then, let us reason together, and try to discover the true light upon all subjects, connected with our temporal or eternal happiness.[2]

4

WAS THE *BOOK OF MORMON* PRODUCED BY OCCULT METHODS?

Even though the Mormon church claims that Joseph Smith translated the "gold plates" (containing the "historical" records of the Nephites and Lamanites) by the power of God using divine implements called the Urim and Thummim,[3] the *Book of Mormon* was actually produced through psychic methods and has nothing to do with ancient history. It is a product of nineteenth-century occultism. (See also Questions 11 [p. 45], 19 [p. 77].)

Historical documents indicate that when Smith translated the *Book of Mormon* he was engaging in his usual practice of crystal gazing. The testimonies of David Whitmer (one of the three key "witnesses" to the *Book of Mormon*), Emma Smith (one of Joseph Smith's wives and scribes), and William Smith (Joseph's brother) make this clear.

In 1877, Whitmer acknowledged that the alleged "Egyptian" characters on the gold plates (Nephi 1:2) and their English interpretation appeared to Joseph Smith while using his seer stone with his face buried inside a hat:

> I will now give you a description of the manner in which the *Book of Mormon* was translated. Joseph Smith would put the seer stone into a hat, and put his face in the hat, drawing it closely around his face to exclude the light; and in the darkness the spiritual light would shine. A piece of something resembling parchment would appear, and on that appeared the writing. One character at a time would appear, and under it was the interpretation in English. Brother Joseph would read off the English to Oliver Cowdery, who was his principal scribe, and when it was written down and repeated to Brother Joseph to see if it was correct, then it would disappear, and another character with the interpretation would appear. Thus the *Book of Mormon* was translated....[4]

Emma Smith revealed the same occult method: "In writing for your father, I frequently wrote day after day....He sitting with his face buried in his hat, with the stone in it, and dictating hour after hour with nothing between us."[5]

Clearly, the *Book of Mormon* was produced through a form of occult crystal gazing. Testimonies such as these (and others)[6] have brought even some Mormons who reject the idea to at least concede its possibility. The tenth president and prophet, Joseph Fielding Smith, confessed in his *Doctrines of Salvation* that "it may have been so."[7]

5

DO HUMAN SOURCES IN THE *BOOK OF MORMON* DISQUALIFY ITS CLAIMS TO DIVINE REVELATION?

The Mormon church believes that the *Book of Mormon* is an account of ancient writings first inscribed on gold plates at least 1500 years ago that chronicled the history of the so-called "Nephite" and "Lamanite" peoples, who spanned a period from 600 B.C.–A.D. 421. Thus the *Book of Mormon* is purportedly a translation of ancient historical records that date at least 1400 years before Joseph Smith was born. Mormons maintain that apart from divine revelation it would have been impossible for Joseph Smith to have done such a translation. They consider the book a great proof of its heavenly derivation. Mormons, however, rarely consider the other possibilities that explain the origin of the *Book of Mormon* far better. For example, it could have been a combination of Smith's natural talent and spiritistic revelation from crystal gazing. Concerning the former, there are several possible human sources for the *Book of Mormon.*

Fawn Brodie, who was excommunicated from the Mormon church for her scholarly critical study on Joseph Smith, *No Man Knows My History: The Life of Joseph Smith,*[8] cites persuasive evidence for a nineteenth-century origin of the *Book of Mormon.* For example, how likely is it that Jewish writers between 600 B.C.–A.D. 421 would discuss the social and religious issues common to nineteenth-century Christian America? As Brodie asks:

> Any theory of the origin of the *Book of Mormon* that spotlights the prophet [alone] and blacks out the stage on which he performed is certain to be a distortion.
>
> [For example, in] the speeches of the Nephi prophets one may find [discussions of] the religious conflicts that were splitting the churches in the 1820's. Alexander Campbell, founder of the Disciples of Christ, wrote in the first able review of the *Book of Mormon:* "This prophet Smith, through his stone spectacles, wrote on the plates of Nephi,

> in his *Book of Mormon,* every error and almost every truth discussed in New York for the last ten years. He decided all the great [religious] controversies...[and even the questions of] Freemasonry, Republican government and the rights of man. But he is better skilled in the controversies in New York than in the geography or history of Judea. He makes John baptize in the village of Bethabara and says Jesus was born in Jerusalem.
>
> The theology of the *Book of Mormon,* like its anthropology, was only a potpourri....Always an eclectic, Joseph never exhausted any theory he had appropriated. He seized a fragment here and another there and of the odd assortment built his history.[9]

Various researchers such as David Persuitte (*Joseph Smith and the Origins of the Book of Mormon*) and Hal Hougey (*A Parallel, The Basis of the Book of Mormon*) have pointed out a number of striking similarities between the *Book of Mormon* and Ethan Smith's 1823 text, *View of the Hebrews,* a book that was available to Joseph Smith.[10] Parallels between the *Book of Mormon* and *View of the Hebrews* were sufficient enough to prompt no less an authority than Mormon historian B.H. Roberts to study the issue. He concluded that it was possible for Joseph Smith alone to have written the *Book of Mormon.*[11]

Many scriptures from the King James Bible, first published in A.D. 1611 can somehow be found in the *Book of Mormon,* which was supposedly written a thousand years earlier. According to Dr. Anthony Hoekema, there are some 27,000 words taken from the King James Bible. Anyone who compares the following list, which includes just several examples, will see that Smith copied material from the King James Bible (including translation errors, see, e.g., Isaiah 4:5; 5:25 and 2 Nephi 14:5; 15:25):

> 1 Nephi chapters 20,21—Isaiah chapters 48,49
>
> 2 Nephi chapters 7,8—Isaiah chapters 50,51
>
> 2 Nephi chapters 12,24—Isaiah chapters 2–14

Mosiah chapter 14—Isaiah chapter 53

3 Nephi chapters 12,14—Matthew chapters 5–7

3 Nephi chapter 22—Isaiah chapter 54

3 Nephi chapters 24,25—Malachi chapters 3,4

Moroni chapter 10—1 Corinthians 12:1-11[12]

Jerald and Sandra Tanner, who have done large amounts of research on Mormonism, have also supplied evidence for other sources for the creation of the *Book of Mormon*, including Josiah Priest's *The Wonders of Nature and Providence Displayed* (Albany, NY: 1825); *The Wayne Sentinel; The Apocrypha*, a dream of Joseph Smith's father; and *The Westminster Confession* and *Catechism.*

Dr. Thomas J. Finley, an expert in Semitics and Western Akkadian concluded his own study of the *Book of Mormon* as follows: "There is no solid evidence that the *Book of Mormon* was written by Nephites in ancient times. Contrary evidence makes it more likely that the book is a product of Joseph Smith's time, with the KJV strongly influencing it....We have not discovered any features of the *Book of Mormon* that would make plausible the hypothesis that Joseph Smith translated it from ancient gold plates."[13]

Dr. David J. Shepherd is a specialist on ancient translations and the phenomenon of pseudotranslation. He concludes that despite recent LDS attempts to prove otherwise, the *Book of Mormon* is clearly a pseudotranslation and that "it seems quite clear that in producing the *Book of Mormon*, Joseph Smith was demonstrably dependent on source texts that were already extant and available in English."[14]

All this indicates that the *Book of Mormon* was not a translation of ancient records. Numerous scholars, Christian, secular, and LDS, now agree that the *Book of Mormon* is a nineteenth-century creation (for examples, see LDS scholar Mark Thomas, *Digging in Cumorah: Reclaiming Book of Mormon Narratives* and Brent Lee Metcalfe, ed., *New Approaches to the Book of Mormon: Explorations in Critical Methodology*).

What then is the real source of the *Book of Mormon*? The most likely answer is that it combines human sources from other books and spiritistic revelation through Smith's use of the seer stone and other occult methods. From 1825 to 1844, Smith claimed to receive hundreds of direct revelations from the spirit world—from God, Jesus, angels such as "Moroni," New Testament apostles, and others. So unless Smith was lying about all these supernatural encounters, they offer one of the cornerstones upon which the LDS faith was founded. Because Smith was an accomplished occultist (see Question 19), the revelations he received were occult, not divine. Some 135 of these revelations were printed in *Doctrine and Covenants*, the second and doctrinally most important volume of LDS scripture.

6

DOES THE SCIENCE OF ARCHAEOLOGY SUPPORT THE *BOOK OF MORMON*?

If the *Book of Mormon* were truly a historical record of ancient peoples inhabiting a vast civilization, it is probable that at least some archaeological data would confirm the civilization, just as it has confirmed, in varying degrees, biblical and other ancient histories. The *Book of Mormon* claims to represent the history of three different groups of people, all of whom allegedly migrated from the Near East to Central and South America. Two of the groups supposedly traveled as far north as Mexico and North America (the *Book of Mormon*, Ether and 1 Nephi).* The Nephites and Lamanites are said to have been Semitic, with the most important group being led by Lehi of Jerusalem, whose descendants became

* Although the traditional view is that the *Book of Mormon* story covers North and South America, some Brigham Young University academicians, apparently attempting to coordinate *Book of Mormon* claims and geography with existing data backpedal and accept a more limited geography.[15] (They believe, for example, that the Cumorah in New York was really in Southern Mexico.)

the Nephites. The main history of the *Book of Mormon* concerns the Nephites.

Not a shred of archaeological evidence exists to support the idea that the *Book of Mormon's* claims are historical, despite many vigorous archaeological excavations financed by the Mormon church. This has forced many non-Mormon researchers to conclude that the *Book of Mormon* is primarily historical invention. The late Dr. Walter Martin referred to "the hundreds of areas where this book defies reason or common sense."[16] Both the prestigious National Geographic Society and the Bureau of American Ethnology of the Smithsonian Institution have issued various statements denying Mormon claims, and Jerald and Sandra Tanner's book *Archaeology and the Book of Mormon,* and other works, show that archaeological confirmation claimed by the Mormon church is untrustworthy.[17]

The National Geographic wrote in 1998, "Archaeologists and other scholars have long probed the hemisphere's past, and the Society does not know of anything found so far that has substantiated the Book of Mormon." In 1996, the Smithsonian's Department of Anthropology issued a formal statement, "Smithsonian archaeologists see no direct connection between the archaeology of the New World and the subject matter of the book."[18]

Nevertheless, Mormon apologists and lay writers alike claim archaeology proves the *Book of Mormon* is true. In fact, this is a standard argument frequently used by Mormon missionaries in their attempts to convert others. As Hal Hougey observes in *Archaeology and the Book of Mormon,* most Mormons think archaeology is on their side: "The numerous books and articles by Latter-day Saints over the years have shown that Mormons believe that the fruits of archaeological research may properly be applied to verify the Book of Mormon. Dr. Ross T. Christensen, a Mormon anthropologist, agrees: 'If the book's history is fallacious, its doctrine cannot be genuine....I am fully confident that the nature of the Book is such that a definitive archaeological test can be applied to it.'"[19]

But definitive archaeological tests have already been applied, and they have discredited the *Book of Mormon* as history. Consider two final examples. Brigham Young University archaeology professor Raymond T. Matheny worked in the area of Mesoamerican archaeology for 22 years, and concluded that the scientific data do not support LDS claims: "I have felt that Mormons...have been grasping at straws for a very long time." "I would say in evaluating the Book of Mormon that it has no place in the New World whatsoever." The respected Mesoamerican archaeologist Michael Coe agreed: "The bare facts of the matter are that nothing, absolutely nothing, has ever shown up in any New World excavation which would suggest to a dispassionate observer that the Book of Mormon, as claimed by Joseph Smith, is a historical document relating to the history of early immigrants to our hemisphere."[20]

7

HOW CREDIBLE IS THE MANUSCRIPT EVIDENCE FOR THE *BOOK OF MORMON*?

Another problem with Mormon claims about ancient Nephite history is the lack of manuscript evidence. Because of their perceived importance, the religious scriptures of most ancient peoples have been preserved, despite the sometimes incredible odds against it. Rarely, the preservation is almost perfect, and the Bible of the Jews and the New Testament of the Christians are unique in this regard.[21]

While the manuscript evidence for the Bible is rich and abundant, for the Mormon scriptures it is nonexistent.[22] There is no textual evidence for either an ancient *Book of Mormon* or for any of Smith's other alleged ancient records. The "records of the Nephites," for instance, were never cited by any ancient writer, nor are there any known manuscripts or even fragments of manuscripts in existence older than the ones dictated by Joseph Smith in the late 1820s. Joseph Smith's "Book of Moses" is likewise without documentary support. The only handwritten manuscripts for the "Book of Moses" are those dictated by Joseph Smith in the early 1830s. The "Book of Abraham" purports to be a translation of an ancient Egyptian papyrus that Smith had purchased and was later lost. However, once found, the original papyrus was discovered to be an Egyptian "Book of Breathings" that has nothing to do with Abraham or his religion. Therefore, we have no evidence for the "Book of Abraham" prior to Joseph Smith's "translation." It would appear, then, that there is no documentary evidence for any of Joseph Smith's scriptural works that date prior to the late 1820s.[23]

Despite recent LDS/Foundation for Ancient Research and Mormon Studies (FARMS) research attempting to prove the legitimacy of the "Book of Abraham," scholarly research—secular and LDS—continues to disprove current claims. (See Questions 25, 27.) This demonstrates that the "Book of Abraham" is a forgery and that the Mormon Church continues to deceive the faithful as to the true nature of this alleged scripture, not to mention the others. Robert K. Ritner taught Egyptology at Yale and is an associate professor of Egyptology at the University of Chicago. He is an authority in the kind of late Egyptian hieratic documents involved. Edward H. Ashment is the former Coordinator for Translation Services, Church of Jesus Christ of Latter-day Saints, and a doctoral candidate in Egyptology at the University of Chicago. They are two of the many voices that show Smith's claims were entirely false.[24]

8

DOES THE *BOOK OF MORMON* TEACH MORMON DOCTRINES?

A further point, briefly made here but which should be of particular interest to many Mormons, is that Mormon teachings are not principally derived from the *Book of Mormon.* Mormon doctrine is derived primarily from another Mormon scripture, *Doctrine and Covenants* (*D&C*).

The dilemma this poses for the Mormon church is a serious one because *D&C* emphasizes that the *Book of Mormon* contains basic, or fundamental, Mormon teachings. For example, according to *D&C*, the *Book of Mormon* contains "the truth and the Word of God" (*D&C*, 19:26); "the fullness of the gospel of Jesus Christ" (that is, Mormon teachings, *D&C*, 20:9); and "the *fullness* of the *everlasting* gospel" (*D&C*, 135:3). *Doctrine and Covenants* also has Jesus claiming that the *Book of Mormon* has "the principles of my gospel" (*D&C*, 42:12), and "*all things written* concerning the foundation of my church, my gospel, and my rock" (*D&C*, 18:4, cf. 17:1-6; emphasis added; see also *Book of Mormon*, Introduction).

According to *Doctrine and Covenants*, then, the *Book of Mormon* must contain at the very least most of the central doctrines of Mormon faith. But the *Book of Mormon* contains few major Mormon teachings. It does not teach any of the following central Mormon principles that form the foundation of the Mormon church and its "gospel": polytheism; God as the product of an eternal progression; eternal marriage; polygamy; human deification; the Trinity as three separate gods; baptism for the dead; maintaining genealogical records; universalism; God once being a man and having a physical body; that God organized, rather than created, the world; mother gods (heavenly mothers); temple marriage as a requirement for exaltation; the concept of eternal intelligences; three degrees of heavenly glory (telestial, terrestrial, celestial); salvation after death in the spirit world; a New Testament era of Mormon organizational offices and functions such as the Melchizedek and Aaronic priesthoods; stake president and first presidency.[25] All this is why some Mormon writers have noted the theological irrelevance of the *Book of Mormon* to Mormonism. For example, John H. Evans observed "how little the whole body of belief of the Latter-day Saints really depends on the revelation of the Nephite record [the *Book of Mormon*]."[26]

Given the vast amounts of scholarly research that is similar to and affirms our brief survey, the unavoidable conclusion is that the *Book of Mormon* is really a piece of nineteenth-century invention. Whatever else it is, it cannot be a divine revelation. This explains why Mormon leaders tell potential converts to ignore criticism of the *Book of Mormon* and rely wholly upon subjective (completely personal) "confirmation" by praying over whether the book is true.[27] Nevertheless, the church's appeal to subjectivity does nothing to convince a rational person why he or she should believe in the *Book of Mormon.* To believe without any evidence is troublesome enough; to believe in spite of the evidence is folly—prayer or no prayer.

SECTION III
CONTRADICTIONS AND FALSE PROPHECIES IN MORMON SCRIPTURES

9

ARE THERE CONTRADICTIONS IN MORMON DOCTRINES?

> *We receive continuing guidance from inspired leaders chosen by the Lord. Through these leaders, the Lord speaks to us and ensures that the true gospel of Jesus Christ is taught.*
>
> —***Membership in the Kingdom, Discussion 6, 8***

According to the Bible, God is a perfect being who is eternal, infinite, immutable, faithful, loving, true, omniscient, just, holy, and righteous. A revelation from God would, therefore, have to be considered internally consistent and without error. Claimed revelations that have conflicting teachings, unresolvable disagreements, errors, and false predictions could not logically be considered to have originated from such a God.

Mormons claim they have additional scripture as well as "Latter-day prophets" to help them correctly understand "doctrines that have confused apostate Christianity for centuries."[1] The late president and prophet of the Mormon church Ezra Taft Benson emphasized that "the [Mormon] gospel encompasses all truth; it is consistent, without conflict, eternal."[2] Mormon scholar

Hugh Nibley states, "Of all churches in the world only this one has not found it necessary to readjust any part of doctrine in the last hundred years."[3] Mormons repeatedly claim that their scriptures are not contradictory,[4] and that the continuing divine revelation received is consistent with earlier revelation.

Why then, when early and modern Mormon teachings are carefully compared, does one discover serious doctrinal contradictions on many key issues, as well as numerous errors and false prophecies? Why have church leaders had "to go back and rework, rewrite, cover-up, change, delete and add [material throughout] all of their books—their histories, their Scriptures? They [also] suppress their diaries because these things show the confusion and the man-made nature of their theology and religion."[5]

Because Mormon theology is replete with contradictions, the church has understandably but inexcusably attempted to suppress information that it has found embarrassing in order to portray a semblance of consistency. (This includes the Reorganized Church, now known as the Community of Christ.)[6] Church leaders have apparently felt this approach was justified for at least two reasons. One is that the real Joseph Smith is *not* a person the church desires to present to the world, hence suppression of true biographical data was necessary. For example, "Joseph Smith had at least 33 wives, twelve of whom were already married with living husbands."[7] The other reason is that modern Mormonism rejects many of its earlier prophets' divinely revealed teachings, and its earlier prophets would reject as false many of the teachings now approved by church leadership. Thus, if the logic of a claim to divine revelation were to be maintained, suppression of contrary data would be necessary. As is typical, the effort failed and much research now exists documenting the fraudulent exercises.[8]

Of course, the contradictions in the LDS scriptures themselves could hardly be suppressed, but had to be reinterpreted in some "acceptable" manner. For example, the *Book of Mormon* teaches there is only one God: "See that ye remember these things; for he said there is but one God..." (Alma 11:35); "...unto the Father, and unto the Son, and unto the Holy Ghost, which are one God..." (Mormon 7:7). Yet *D&C* 132:20 teaches there are many gods, for example, "Then shall they be gods, because they have all power, and the angels are subject unto them." The LDS "solution" is to claim there is only one true (principal) God, among many "lesser" gods. Regardless, the charts on the following pages provide just a fraction of the many verbatim contradictions found within Mormon teachings.[9]

Verbatim Contradictions in Mormon Doctrine

THE DOCTRINE OF POLYGAMY	
Plural marriage is not essential to salvation or exaltation (Bruce McConkie, *Mormon Doctrine*, 578).	For behold, I reveal unto you a new and everlasting covenant; and if ye abide not [in] that covenant, then are ye damned; for no one can reject this covenant and be permitted to enter into my glory (*D&C*, 132:4).
THE NUMBER OF GODS	
Now Zeezrom said: Is there more than one God? And he answered, No (*Book of Mormon*, Alma 11:28-29).	There are three Gods—the Father, the Son, and the Holy Ghost (Bruce McConkie, *Mormon Doctrine*, 317).
ADAM IN THE GARDEN	
The *Book of Mormon*, the Bible, *Doctrine and Covenants*, and *The Pearl of Great Price* all declare that Adam's body was created from the dust of the ground, that is, from the dust of this ground, this earth (Joseph Fielding Smith, *Doctrines of Salvation*, 1:90).	Adam was made from the dust of an earth, but not from the dust of this earth (Brigham Young, *Journal of Discourses*, 3:319).
When our father Adam came into the Garden of Eden, he came into it with a celestial body (Brigham Young, *Journal of Discourses*, 1:50).	We hear a lot of people talk about Adam passing through mortality and the resurrection on another earth and then coming here to live and die again. Well, that is a contradiction of the word of the Lord, for a resurrected being does not die.... Adam had not passed through a resurrection when he was in the Garden of Eden (Joseph Fielding Smith, *Doctrines of Salvation*, 1:91).
THE OMNISCIENCE AND OMNIPOTENCE OF GOD	
Each of these personal Gods has equal knowledge with all the rest....None of these Gods are progressing in knowledge: neither can they progress in the acquirement of any truth.... Some have gone so far as to say that all the Gods	We might ask, when shall we cease to learn? I will give you my opinion about it; never never... both in time and eternity (Brigham Young, *Journal of Discourses*, 3:203).

Verbatim Contradictions cont.

were progressing in truth, and would continue to progress to all eternity…but let us examine, for a moment, the absurdity of such a conjecture (Orson Pratt, *The Seer,* Aug. 1853, 117).	God is not progressing in knowledge (McConkie, *Mormon Doctrine,* 1966, 239).
Do not…say that he cannot learn anymore… (Brigham Young, *Deseret Weekly News,* 22:309).	[God has] knowledge of all things…(Joseph Smith, *Lectures on Faith,* 44, cited in McConkie, *Mormon Doctrine,* 545).
[The teaching that] God is progressing or increasing in any of these attributes, [knowledge, faith, power, justice, judgment, mercy, truth is] false heresy (McConkie, *Mormon Doctrine,* 263).	God…is not advancing in knowledge.…He is increasing in power (Joseph Fielding Smith, as cited in Joseph W. Musser, *Michael Our Father and Our God,* 27).
THE FALL OF MAN	
That old serpent that did beguile our first parents, which was the cause of their fall; which was the cause of all mankind becoming carnal, sensual, devilish, knowing evil from good, subjecting themselves to the devil. Thus all mankind were lost (*Book of Mormon,* Mosiah 16:3,4). For the natural man is an enemy to God, and has been from the fall of Adam, and will be, forever and ever, unless he yields to the enticings of the Holy Spirit (Mosiah 3:19). [God] showed unto all men that they were lost, because of the transgression of their parents (*Book of Mormon,* 2 Nephi 2:21).	In the true gospel of Jesus Christ there is no original sin (John Widstoe, *Evidences and Reconciliation,* 195, in Cowan, *Mormon Claims,* 75).
TREATMENT OF ENEMIES	
As I remarked, we were then very pious, and we prayed the Lord to kill the mob (Apostle George A. Smith, *Journal of Discourses,* 5:107). (Cf. the discussion of blood atonement, etc., in *Behind the Mask of Mormonism,* chapter 2, 28.)	But behold I say unto you, love your enemies, bless them that curse you, do good to them that hate you and pray for them who despitefully use you and persecute you; that ye may be the children of your Father who is in heaven (*Book of Mormon,* 3 Nephi 12:44,45).
THE INDWELLING OF GOD	
The Lord hath said…in the hearts of the righteous doth he dwell (*Book of Mormon,* Alma 34:36).	The idea that the Father and the Son dwell in a man's heart is an old sectarian notion, and is false (*D&C,* 130:3).
SALVATION BY GRACE	
Remember, after ye are reconciled to God, that it is only in and through the grace of God that ye are saved (*Book of Mormon,* 2 Nephi 10:24).	Fulfilling the commandments bringeth remission of sins (*Book of Mormon,* Moroni 8:25). Except ye shall keep my commandments…ye shall in no case enter into the kingdom of heaven (*Book of Mormon,* 3 Nephi 12:20).

Verbatim Contradictions cont.

GOD'S IMMUTABILITY	
Mormon prophets have continuously taught the sublime truth that God the Eternal Father was once a mortal man (M.R. Hunter, *Gospel Through the Ages*, 104).	Behold I say unto you, he that denieth these things knoweth not the gospel of Christ; yea, he has not read the Scriptures; if so, he does not understand them. For do we not read that God is the same yesterday, today, and forever, and in him there is no variableness neither shadow or changing? And now if ye have imagined up unto yourselves a god who doth vary, and in whom there is shadow of changing, then have ye imagined up unto yourselves a god who is not a God of miracles (*Book of Mormon*, Mormon 9:8-10).
THE CREATION OF MAN	
God...created man, as we create our children; for there is no other process of creation in heaven, on the earth, in the earth, or under the earth, or in all the eternities that is, that were, or that ever will be (Brigham Young, *Journal of Discourses*, 11:122).	By the power of his word man came upon the face of the earth which earth was created by the power of his word. Wherefore, if God being able to speak and the world was, and to speak and man was created, O then, why is he not able to command the earth or the workmanship of his hands upon the face of it, according to his will and pleasure? (*Book of Mormon*, Jacob 4:9).
THE FALL PRODUCING CHILDREN	
If Adam had not transgressed he would not have fallen....And they would have had no children (*Book of Mormon*, 2 Nephi 2:22,23). Were it not for our transgressions we never should have had seed (*The Pearl of Great Price*, Moses 5:11).	And I, God, created man in mine own image. ...Male and female created I them. And I, God, blessed them, and said unto them: Be fruitful and multiply (*The Pearl of Great Price*, Moses 2:27, 28).
CHILD BAPTISM	
And their children shall be baptized for the remission of their sins when eight years old (*D&C*, 68:27).	Listen to the words of Christ...your Lord and God....I know that it is solemn mockery before God, that ye should baptize little children.... Yea, teach parents that they must repent and be baptized (*Book of Mormon*, Moroni 8:8-10).

The modern Mormon has no logical solution to the problems that such changes in doctrine present, and the response of church leadership has, unfortunately, not been gracious. Noted Associated Press writer Richard N. Ostling, former senior correspondent for *Time* and one of the premier religion reporters in the country, points out some church problems that help explain the quandary: "centralized control, continuing secrecy, regimentation,...suspicion toward intellectuals, suppression of open discussion, file-keeping on members for disciplinary use, sporadic purges of malcontents, [and] church education as indoctrination."[10]

10

ARE THERE CONTRADICTIONS BETWEEN THE BIBLE'S TEACHINGS AND MORMON DOCTRINES?

A more serious problem for a church that claims to be Bible-based is the clear contradiction between Mormon doctrine and the Bible. Hundreds of contrasts could be given. The following chart, "Contradictions Between Mormon Doctrine and Biblical Truth," lists several.

Contradictions Between Mormon Doctrine and Biblical Truth

THE GATES OF HELL PREVAILED	
The gates of hell have prevailed and will continue to prevail over the Catholic Mother of Harlots, and over *all* her Protestant Daughters (*Pamphlets* by Orson Pratt, 112, cited by Jerald and Sandra Tanner, *Changing World*, 27). The kingdoms of this world made war against the kingdom of God...and they prevailed against it. ...[It has been] overcome and nothing is left (Orson Pratt, *Journal of Discourses*, 13:125).	I will build my church, and the gates of Hades will not overcome it (Matthew 16:18).
JUSTIFICATION BY POLYGAMY	
Abraham received concubines, and they bore him children; and it was accounted unto him for righteousness (*D&C*, 132:37).	For what does the Scripture say? "Abraham believed God, and it was credited to him as righteousness" (Romans 4:3).

Contradictions cont.

JUSTIFICATION BY WORKS	
Man is justified by works (McConkie, *Doctrinal New Testament Commentary,* 3:260).	For we maintain that a man is justified by faith apart from observing the law (Romans 3:28). By the works of the Law no flesh will be justified in His sight (Romans 3:20 NASB).
HATRED OF ENEMIES	
In Missouri we were taught to "pray for our enemies, that *God would damn them, and give us power to kill them*" (Letter, B.F. Johnson, 1903, cited in Jerald and Sandra Tanner, *The Changing World of Mormonism,* p. 485; see *Journal of Discourses* 5:32,95,107,133; 7:122 for similar examples).	You have heard that it was said, "YOU SHALL LOVE YOUR NEIGHBOR, and hate your enemy." But I say to you, love your enemies and pray for those who persecute you (Matthew 5:43-44 NASB). Do not repay anyone evil for evil. Be careful to do what is right in the eyes of everybody (Romans 12:17).
MAN AS INHERENTLY GOOD	
It is, however, universally received by professors of religion as a Scriptural doctrine that man is naturally opposed to God. This is not so. Paul says in his Epistle to the Corinthians, "But the natural man receiveth not the things of God." But I say it is the unnatural "man that receiveth not the things of God."... *The natural man is of God* (Brigham Young, *Journal of Discourses,* 9:305).	But a natural man does not accept the things of the Spirit of God, for they are foolishness to him; and he cannot understand them, because they are spiritually appraised (1 Corinthians 2:14 NASB). So this I say, and affirm together with the Lord, that you walk no longer just as the Gentiles also walk, in the futility of their mind, being darkened in their understanding, excluded from the life of God because of the ignorance that is in them, because of the hardness of their heart (Ephesians 4:17-18 NASB).
It is not natural for men to be evil (John Taylor, 3rd President, *Journal of Discourses,* 10:50).	As it is written: "There is no one righteous, not even one; there is no one who understands, no one who seeks God. All have turned away, they have together become worthless; there is no one who does good, not even one" (Romans 3:10–12).
NO ORIGINAL SIN	
In the true gospel of Jesus Christ there is no original sin (John Widtsoe, *Evidences and Reconciliations,* 195, in Cowan, *Mormon Claims,* 75).	One trespass was condemnation for all men (Romans 5:18).

Contradictions cont.

REJECTION OF CHRIST'S DEITY	
Jesus *became* a God...through consistent effort (M.R. Hunter, *Gospel Through the Ages*, Salt Lake City: *Deseret*, 1945, 51, in McElveen, *Will the "Saints" Go Marching In?* 154).	The Word was God (John 1:1). Jesus Christ is the same yesterday and today and forever (Hebrews 13:8). His goings forth are from long ago, from the days of eternity (Micah 5:2 NASB).
THE INDWELLING OF GOD	
The idea that the Father and the Son dwell in a man's heart is an old sectarian notion, and is false (*D&C*, 130:3).	Jesus answered and said to him, "If anyone loves Me, he will keep My word; and My Father will love him, and We will come to him, and make Our abode with him" (John 14:23 NASB).
ADAM AS GOD	
Adam is our Father and Our God (Brigham Young, *Journal of Discourses*, 1:50).	Then to Adam He said, "...you are dust, and to dust you shall return" (Genesis 3:17,19).
SOURCE OF SALVATION	
There is no salvation outside the Church of Jesus Christ of Latter-day Saints (McConkie, *Mormon Doctrine*, 670).	Yet to all who received him, to those who believed in his name, he gave the right to become children of God (John 1:12). Whoever believes in the Son has eternal life, but whoever rejects the Son will not see life, for God's wrath remains on him (John 3:36).
THE HOLY SPIRIT AND BAPTISM	
Cornelius...could not receive the gift of the Holy Ghost until after he was baptized (Joseph Smith, *Teachings of the Prophet Joseph Smith*, comp. Joseph Fielding Smith, 1977, p. 199).	Cornelius received "the gift of the Holy Spirit" before he was baptized (Acts 10:43-48).
THE CREATION	
There really was no beginning because God and matter are eternal (Wallace, *Can Mormonism Be Proven Experimentally?* 163).	In the beginning God created the heavens and the earth (Genesis 1:1).

The LDS church attemps to foster a reputation for honesty and integrity. If so, how does it logically explain its underhanded approach to both its own scriptures and its claim to be a faith consistant with biblical teaching? As we will see, what has been discussed so far is only the tip of the iceburg.

11

WAS JOSEPH SMITH A TRUE PROPHET OF GOD?

> *The only way of ascertaining a true prophet is to compare his prophecies with the ancient Word of God, and see if they agree, and if they do and come to pass, then certainly he is a true prophet....When, therefore any man,* no matter who, *or how high his standing may be, utters, or publishes, anything that afterwards proves to be untrue,* he is a false prophet.[11]
>
> —Joseph Smith

Another vital area relative to Mormon claims is the Church's prophetic record. The many false prophecies found throughout its history, beginning with Joseph Smith, further prove that Mormonism cannot be founded on divine revelation. While we have not examined every Mormon prophecy, the many we did study proved counterfeit. We include several here, which are typical of what one finds.

1. *Joseph Smith's Canadian prophecy.* David Whitmer (one of the three principal witnesses to the writing of the *Book of Mormon*) tells a highly relevant story that reveals Joseph Smith to be a false prophet. Here are Whitmer's own words:

> When the Book of Mormon was in the hands of the printer, more money was needed to finish the printing of it....Brother Hyrum said it had been suggested to him that some of the brethren might go to Toronto, Canada and sell the copyright of the Book of Mormon for considerable money: and he persuaded Joseph to inquire of the Lord about it. Joseph concluded to do so. He had not yet given up the [seer] stone. Joseph looked into the hat in which he placed the stone, and *received a revelation* that some of the brethren should go to Toronto, Canada, *and that they would sell the copyright* of the Book of Mormon. Hyrum Page and Oliver Cowdery went to Toronto on this mission,

but *they failed entirely to sell the copyright*, returning without any money. Joseph was at my father's house when they returned. I was there also, and am *an eyewitness* to these facts. Jacob Whitmer and John Whitmer were also present when Hyrum Page and Oliver Cowdery returned from Canada.

Well, we were all in great trouble; and we asked Joseph how it was that he had received a revelation from the Lord for some brethren to go to Toronto and sell the copyright and the brethren had utterly failed in their undertaking. Joseph did not know how it was, so he inquired of the Lord about it, and behold the following revelation came through the stone:

> *Some revelations are of God: some revelations are of man: and some revelations are of the devil.*

So we see that the revelation to go to Toronto and sell the copyright was not of God [even though Smith claimed it was], but was of the devil or of the heart of man....This was a lesson for our benefit *and we should have profited by it in [the] future more than we did.*

Whitmer concludes his discussion with a warning to every living Mormon:

> Remember this matter brethren; it is very important.... Now is it wisdom to put your trust in Joseph Smith, and believe all his revelations in the *Doctrine and Covenants* to be of God?...I will say here, that I could tell you *other false revelations* that came through Brother Joseph as mouthpiece (not through the stone), but this will suffice. Many of Brother Joseph's revelations were never printed. The revelation to go to Canada was written down on paper, but was never printed.[12]

2. *The "City and Temple" prophecy*. In a revelation given to Joseph Smith on September 22 and 23, 1832, "The word of the Lord" declared that both a city and a temple are to be built "in the

western boundaries of the state of Missouri" (that is, in Independence, Missouri):

> A revelation of Jesus Christ unto his servant Joseph Smith, Jun[ior]....*Yea, the word of the Lord* concerning his church ...for the gathering of his saints to stand upon Mount Zion, which shall be the city of New Jerusalem. Which *city shall be built,* beginning at the temple lot...*in the western boundaries of the state of Missouri,* and dedicated by the hand of Joseph Smith....Verily *this is the word of the Lord,* that the city New Jerusalem shall be built by the gathering of saints, beginning at this place, even the place of the temple, which temple shall be reared *in this generation. For verily this generation shall not all pass away* until an house shall be built unto the Lord, and a cloud shall rest upon it, which cloud shall be even the glory of the Lord, which shall fill the house....Therefore, as I said concerning the sons of Moses—for the sons of Moses and also *the sons of Aaron shall offer an acceptable offering and sacrifice in the house of the Lord,* which house shall be built under the Lord in this generation, upon the consecrated spot as *I have appointed* (*D&C,* 84:1-5,31, emphasis added).

This prophecy clearly teaches that a temple and a city will be built in western Missouri in the generation of the people then living and that it will be dedicated by the hand of Joseph Smith himself. This temple will stand (in western Missouri) "upon Mount Zion" and the city will be named "the city of New Jerusalem." It was to be the place Christ returned to at His Second Coming.[13]

In *Doctrine and Covenants* 97:19 (August 1833) and 101:17-21 (December 1833), "God" declares that He is absolutely certain as to His intent and the location of this temple: "Zion cannot fall, nor be moved out of her place, for God is there, and the hand of the Lord is there," and "there is none other place appointed than that which I have appointed; neither shall there be any other place." Interestingly, on July 20, 1833, when Smith was giving this particular prophecy in Kirtland, Ohio, unaware of events occurring in Missouri, the Mormon community had already agreed to leave Missouri because of "persecution." In other words, even as Smith was giving the prophecy "in the name of the Lord," "Zion" was already being "moved out of her place."[14]

In spite of the numerous ways that Mormon leaders have tried to justify the "City and Temple" prophecy since it was made, more than 170 years have passed and neither the temple nor the city has been built. There is no way to escape the conclusion that this is a false prophecy. But since Mormonism assumes that Joseph Smith was a true prophet, it cannot be a false prophecy, so a process of rationalization sets in. For example, Joseph Fielding Smith dealt with the "generation problem" by claiming that the term "generation" meant an indefinite period of time, and that due to "persecution" God had "absolved the saints and postponed the day."[15] Now everyone could relax—there never was a false prophecy after all.

3. *The "Second Coming" prophecy.* Along with Jehovah's Witnesses and Seventh-day Adventists, Joseph Smith predicted that the Second Coming of Christ would occur in the latter part of the nineteenth century. In his *History of the Church,* Smith taught that the Second Coming would occur between 1890 and 1891. In 1835 he declared that Christ's return would occur 56 years later, and in 1843 that it would occur in 48 years. Smith claimed that the generation then living would not die "till Christ comes."[16] For example, under the date of April 6, 1843, in his *original History* (taken from Smith's diary, March 10, 1843 to July 14, 1843), one can read: "I prophecy [sic] *in the name of the Lord God*—& let it be written: that the Son of Man will not come in the heavens until I am 85 years old, 48 years hence or about 1890."[17] Smith, however, was dead within a year, and Christ still has not returned.

Some of the 12 Mormon apostles were told that they also would remain until Christ returned. For example, the Tanners note that Lyman E. Johnson was told that he would "see the Savior come and stand upon the earth with power and great glory" and William Smith was told that he would "be preserved and remain on the earth, until Christ shall come."[18] Because of such a strong belief in the imminence of the Second Coming, Apostle Parley P. Pratt wrote in 1838, "I will state as a prophesy [sic], that there will not be an unbelieving Gentile upon this continent 50 years hence; and if they are not greatly scourged, and in a great measure overthrown, within five or ten years from this date, then the Book of Mormon will have proved itself false."[19] Not unexpectedly, the prophecy has been deleted from the modern versions of the *Writings of Parley P. Pratt.*

There have been many other false prophecies throughout the history of the Mormon church, far too numerous to cite here.[20] These include prophecies given to Mormon individuals that were never fulfilled, such as Brigham Young would become president of the United States, a Smith prophecy about the complete overthrow of the U.S. government, and the obviously false 1832 "Civil War" prophecy in *Doctrine and Covenants,* 87:1-8, which would lead to global war and the end of the world.

With so many false prophecies by Smith and other Mormons, one is tempted to assume that they were either carried away by false visions of their own mind or through spiritistic duplicity. Certainly, a truthful God could not be the author of false predictions. In spite of these falsehoods, many Mormons do not show much concern with them. Apparently this is because they have never come to grips with the biblical teaching on what God requires of a true prophet (Deuteronomy 13; 18; Jeremiah 28:9; Ezekiel 12:28) and what a false prophet really is:

> It is somewhat ironic that most Mormons are basically unimpressed by the evidence against their "prophets" concerning the many false prophecies that have issued forth from them. This behavior is so unusual because of the reverence Mormons give their Presidents as "prophets of God." Their attitude of indifference is primarily based upon ignorance and conditioning. The average Mormon is

> unaware of the biblical tests for a true prophet and is therefore ignorant of how to properly determine if a man is a true prophet or a false prophet. However, the greatest difficulty Mormons have is overcoming their "conditioning." They have been programmed to believe that the greatest test of a prophet is their own personal "testimony" that he is a prophet.[21]

But it must also be said that many Mormons are not even aware of the false prophecies. For example, if one examines the *Doctrine and Covenants Student Manual,* an extensive 500-page commentary on *Doctrine and Covenants,* one finds that the false prophecies are either ignored or carefully reinterpreted.

SECTION IV
MORMONISM AND CHRISTIANITY

12

DOES MORMONISM BELIEVE IN ONE GOD?

Jesus emphasized the importance of knowing the one true God. He said, "This is eternal life, that they may know You, the only true God, and Jesus Christ whom You have sent" (John 17:3 NASB). Mormons and Christians both agree that accurate knowledge of God is vital. In this section we will examine the Mormon view of God and contrast it with the Christian (biblical) view to show how distinct and incompatible the two beliefs are.

The Mormon church does emphasize the importance of a correct understanding of God. The LDS *Doctrines of the Gospel* (the student manual used at Brigham Young University for Religion courses 231 and 232) declares: "Central to our faith as Latter-day Saints is a correct understanding of God the Father."[1] The problem is that the Mormon church claims only they understand God accurately; all others are wrong. Joseph Smith testified, "There are but a few beings in the world who understand rightly the character of God."[2] Likewise the leading Mormon theologian James Talmage claimed, "[The] sectarian [Christian] view of the Godhead [contains]...numerous theories and dogmas of men, many of which are utterly incomprehensible in their inconsistency and mysticism."[3]

When Mormons claim that they "believe in the biblical God," what they mean is that they believe that the Bible actually teaches the Mormon concept of God and not the Christian concept. Because of its alleged apostasy, Christianity corrupted the scriptures and lost the true teaching of God; therefore, the historic Christian doctrine of God is not truly biblical. This leaves Mormons free to concede that their concept of deity is contrary to traditional Christian faith, but not the Bible. William O. Nelson, director of the Melchizedek Priesthood Department writes, "Some who write anti-Mormon pamphlets insist that the Latter-day Saint concept of Deity is contrary to what is recognized as traditional Christian doctrine. In this they are quite correct."[4] So the real issue is to ascertain the true biblical teaching on the nature of God. The following chart, "The Nature of God," points out some major differences between the Mormon and biblical/Christian views of God.

The Nature of God

MORMON CONCEPT OF DEITY	BIBLICAL/CHRISTIAN CONCEPT OF DEITY
Material (a physical body of flesh and bones)	Immaterial (spirit)
Mortal, finite	Immortal, infinite
Changeable, evolving	Immutable
Physically localized	Omnipresent
Polygamous or incestuous	Jesus was monogamous (celibate)
Polytheistic	Monotheistic
Tri-theistic (three earth gods)	Trinitarian
Exalted saved man	Eternal deity
Eternally progressing in certain attributes (early Mormonism)	Eternally immutable in all characteristics
Feminine counterpart (heavenly mother)	No feminine counterpart
Adam, once considered God (early Mormonism)	Adam, a creation of God
Jesus, begotten by Elohim's physical intercourse with Mary	Jesus, begotten supernaturally by the Holy Spirit (virgin birth)
Polygamist Jesus (some early Mormons)	Celibate Jesus

The most basic theological contrast between the two faiths is that Christianity is monotheistic, believing in only one God, while Mormonism is polytheistic, believing in many gods—and therefore, can hardly be considered biblical or Christian. Drs. Mosser, Owen, and Beckwith point out that most of the major differences between Mormonism and Christianity stem from the fact that Christianity believes in one creator God while Mormonism believes in a plurality of gods and denies the absolute creation of the world.[5]

Nevertheless, Mormons are very uncomfortable with the charge of polytheism. No less an authority than the late Bruce McConkie categorically insisted that "the saints [Mormons] are not polytheists."[6] Stephen Robinson, chairman of the Department of Ancient Scripture at Brigham Young University and author of *Are Mormons Christians?* (which he emphatically affirms), argues that "the Latter-day Saints [doctrine does not]...constitute genuine polytheism." He takes pains to argue that "the Latter-day Saints [should] be considered worshipers of the one true God."[7]

But if Mormons are in actual fact polytheists, why do they claim they are monotheists? Mormons claim to worship a central deity and thus can claim (however unconvincingly) that they believe in "one God." But this is undeniably not their theology. When Mormons deny the charge of polytheism, they merely illustrate a characteristic feature of Mormon apologetics: equivocation, which involves the ambiguous use of words in order to conceal something. Technically, Mormon theology is "henotheistic," a form of polytheism that stresses worship of a central deity. In Mormonism, the central deity is Elohim, whom Mormons call "God the Father." But henotheism also accepts other deities. In Mormonism the other deities accepted include Jesus, the Holy Ghost, and endless other gods who were once men and who have now been "exalted" by evolving into godhood. Principally, it is through the uncritical acceptance of the statements of church authorities that the LDS faith "believes in one God," and/or by a process of seemingly deliberate self-deception caused by the improper use of words that Mormons believe they are monotheists. The truth is that Mormons are polytheists by any standard definition of the term. Any number of dictionaries, including the *Oxford American Dictionary* and the *Macmillan Dictionary for Students*, define polytheism as "belief in or worship of more than one god."[8]

Polytheism can be plainly seen in the words of Joseph Smith: "In the beginning, the head of the Gods called a council of the Gods; and they came together and concocted a plan to create the world and people in it."[9] Consider also the following excerpts from Smith's new revelation of the Creation account in the Mormon scripture known as *The Pearl of Great Price*, which uses the plural term "Gods" some two dozen times:

> At the beginning…the Gods organized and formed the heavens and the earth….And the Gods called the light Day….And the Gods also said: let there be an expanse in the midst of the waters….And the Gods ordered the expanse, so that it divided the waters….And the Gods called the expanse Heaven….And the Gods pronounced the dry land Earth….And the Gods said: let us prepare the earth to bring forth grass….And the Gods organized the lights in the expanse of the heaven….And the Gods organized the two great lights, the greater light to rule the day, and the lesser light to rule the night….And the Gods set them in the expanse of the heavens….And the Gods organized the earth to bring forth the beasts after their kind…. And the Gods took counsel among themselves and said: let us go down and form man in our image….So the Gods went down to organize man in their own image….And the Gods said: we will bless them….And the Gods said: Behold, we will give them every herb bearing seed….And the Gods formed man from the dust of the ground….And the Gods planted a garden, eastward in Eden….And the Gods took the man and put him in the Garden of Eden….And the Gods said: let us make an help meet for the man.[10]

Who can really believe this is referring to monotheism, a belief in only one God?

Mormon polytheism encompasses two aspects. First there is a predominant "local" polytheism as far as the earth is concerned. That is, the earth has three distinct gods who "rule it." This corresponds to Mormon belief that the biblical Trinity is composed of three separate gods. In *Mormon Doctrine*, Bruce McConkie declares, "There are three Gods—the Father, the Son and the Holy Ghost."[11] The principal deity is the Father, a physical god named "Elohim," said to be the primary and most "advanced" god. Mormonism teaches, "The Father is the supreme member of the Godhead."[12] The Son is the physical God "Jehovah" of the Old Testament: "Jesus Christ is Jehovah, the God of the Old Testament."[13] The Holy Ghost, like the others, is a former man who became a god, although, unlike the Father and the Son, he does not have a concrete physical body but is a man with a spiritual body of matter. These three beings, all former men, are the three gods that Mormons are to concern themselves with. But because Mormonism claims that the endless extra-solar gods are not the church's particular concern, their tritheism is somehow held to constitute a belief in one God.

The second aspect of Mormon polytheism moves beyond the earth. If there are an infinite number of earths, each with its god or gods, then there are an infinite number of gods. Whether or not Mormons on earth are "concerned" with them, they do believe in them. McConkie declares:

> To us, speaking in the proper finite sense, these three [the principal Gods of earth] are the only Gods we worship. But in addition there is an infinite number of holy personages, drawn from worlds without number, who have passed on to exaltation [Godhood] and are thus gods....This doctrine of plurality of Gods is so comprehensive and glorious that it reaches out and embraces every exalted personage [God]. Those who attain exaltation are gods.[14]

Brigham Young declared: "How many Gods there are I do not know, but there never was a time when there were not Gods."[15]

Still, the Bible rejects polytheism in the most straightforward terms. God declares in Isaiah: "Before me no god was formed, nor will there be one after me" (43:10). "I am the first and I am the last; apart from me there is no God....Is there any God besides me?...I know not one" (44:6,8). "I am the LORD, and there is no other; apart from me there is no God....there is no God apart from me" (45:5,21).

From Genesis to Revelation the Bible teaches there is *only one true God.* This means it is not possible that Mormon polytheism can logically be considered biblical teaching. The LDS faithful are unfortunately mistaken when they claim to "believe in the God of the Bible."

13

WHAT DOES MORMONISM BELIEVE ABOUT THE BIBLICAL TRINITY?

Mormonism claims that it believes in the biblical Trinity. Dr. Stephen E. Robinson is former chairman of the Department of Ancient Scripture at Brigham Young University, former director of "Pearl of Great Price" research for the Religious Studies Center, and currently a professor of BYU. He claims that Mormonism believes in the biblical God: "The Latter-day Saints accept unequivocally *all the biblical teachings* on the nature of God."[16] He also claims that Mormons believe in the biblical doctrine of the Trinity: "Latter-day Saints believe in the *biblical* Father, Son, and Holy Ghost."[17] Even more explicitly, "If by 'the doctrine of the Trinity' one means *the New Testament teaching* that there is a Father, a Son, and Holy Ghost, all three of whom are fully divine, then Latter-day Saints *believe in the doctrine of the Trinity.* It's as simple as that. The Latter-day Saints' first Article of Faith, written by Joseph Smith in 1842, states, 'We believe in the God, the Eternal Father, and in His Son, Jesus Christ, and in the Holy Ghost.'"[18]

To the contrary, Mormons do not believe in the biblical Trinity; as noted earlier, they believe in tritheism, three gods for this particular earth. Joseph Smith himself unmistakably taught that the Trinity was comprised of three gods:

> Many men say there is one God; the Father, the Son and the Holy Ghost are only one God. I say that is a strange God anyhow—three in one, and one in three! It is curious organization....All are to be crammed into one God according to sectarianism [Christian faith]. It would make the biggest God in all the world. He would be a wonderfully big God—he would be a giant or a monster.[19]

> I will preach on the plurality of Gods. I have selected this text [Genesis 1:1] for that express purpose. I wish to declare that I have always and in all congregations when I have preached on the subject of the Deity, it has been on the plurality of Gods.[20]

Smith's teaching clearly contradicts 2000 years of unambiguous Christian tradition in which the Christian church has, without a doubt, found the doctrine of the Trinity (*one* God in three Persons) clearly presented in the Bible. This can be seen by anyone who reads the Church Fathers and studies the historic creeds.[21]

14

WAS GOD ONCE A MAN?

Mormonism teaches that God was not God from all eternity. Rather—despite the philosophical "chicken or egg" conundrum involved, it believes that God was once a man who evolved into godhood. And to further complicate matters, there are endless numbers of "gods."

How do people become gods? Mormonism believes that all current gods have attained godhood through the good works they performed when they were finite. Joseph Smith describes the process by which people become gods: "When you climb up a ladder, you must begin at the bottom and ascend, step by step, until you arrive at the top; and so it is with the principles of the Gospel—you must begin with the first, and go on until you learn all the principles of exaltation ["exaltation" is his term for becoming a god]."[22] An official Mormon publication, *Gospel Principles*, cites this passage and then comments, "This is the way our Heavenly Father became a God."[23] It then quotes Joseph Smith's own evaluation of "The First Principle of the Gospel," which is to realize that God the Father was once a man: "It is the first principle of the gospel to know for a certainty the character of God, and to know that we may converse with him as one man converses with another, and that he was once a man like us; yea that God himself, the father of us all, dwelt on an earth, the same as Jesus Christ himself did; and I will show it from the Bible."[24] This same source states unblushingly that "God is a glorified and perfected man…."[25] (See *D&C*, 130:22.)

The Mormon student manual *Doctrines of the Gospel* teaches that "God Himself is an exalted man, perfected, enthroned, and supreme."[26] Dr. Stephen Robinson, who is convinced that Mormonism is Christian, agrees, "It is indisputable that Latter-day Saints believe that God was once a human being and that human beings can become gods." The well-known couplet by Lorenzo Snow, fifth president and prophet of the LDS Church, states, "As man now is, God once was; as God now is, man may be."[27]

But Mormonism is divided on how far the process of divine evolution extends. Historically, the church has been uncertain as to whether the gods continue to evolve forever. Many divinely led Mormon presidents and prophets taught that the gods evolved eternally in power and knowledge, which would never quite make them truly omnipotent and omniscient beings.[28] Thus it is written, "God himself is increasing and progressing in knowledge, power and dominion, and will do so worlds without end."[29] Others, such as Bruce McConkie and early Mormon Apostle

Orson Pratt, believe that "God" is omnipotent and omniscient, although they at times have been rebuked for it.[30]

Mormons, however, are not necessarily up front about such beliefs concerning God. Given such a silly teaching that God was once a man like us, perhaps this is not surprising. This quote is in a review of *Mormon America:*

> In a recent conversation I had with two young Mormon missionaries on this subject, they candidly admitted, "Of course we cannot talk openly about our teaching that God was once a man like us. If we started out with that at the door, no one would let us in." When I questioned the honesty of such an approach they replied, "We have to give people milk before meat."[31]

Even LDS president Gordon B. Hinckley has on several occasions been misleading about the true LDS teachings about God once being a man: "I wouldn't say that....That gets into some pretty deep theology,..."[32]

Whether we accept early or late Mormon teachings, one fact is clear: Mormonism has no concept of God according to the biblical and Christian meaning. The Bible asserts in the clearest terms that God is immutable: God never changes in terms of His being, essence, or attributes. (The incarnation of Jesus Christ is no exclusion; in taking on a sinless human nature, the Second Person of the Godhead did not alter His essential divine nature.) For all eternity God has remained God. God was never originally a man who, incredibly, became God through personal effort. The following scriptures testify that God never changes:

> I the LORD do not change (Malachi 3:6).
>
> The Father...does not change (James 1:17).
>
> God is not a man, that he should lie, nor a son of man, that he should change his mind (Numbers 23:19).
>
> From everlasting to everlasting you are God (Psalm 90:2).

In conclusion, the Mormon god is ultimately a finite deity, not the God of the Bible. As LDS scholar Sterling M. McMurrin, E.E.

Ericksen Distinguished Professor, professor of History, professor of Philosophy of Education, and dean of the Graduate School at the University of Utah concludes in his study, "He is therefore finite rather than absolute."[33] "In its rejection of the classical concept of God as eternal, Mormonism is a most radical digression from traditional theism. This is perhaps its most important departure from familiar Christian orthodoxy, for it would be difficult to overestimate the importance to [Mormon] theology of the doctrine that God is a temporal being."[34]

15

WHAT DOES MORMONISM TEACH ABOUT JESUS CHRIST?

> *There are many who say that Latter-day Saints believe in a "different Jesus" than do other Christians and that we are therefore not "Christian."...We believe in the Jesus of the New Testament, and we believe what the New Testament teaches about Him. We do believe things about Jesus that other Christians do not believe, but that is because we know, through revelation, things about Jesus that others do not know....*[35]
>
> —M. Russell Ballard

> *The traditional Christ of whom they [Christians] speak is not the Christ of whom I speak.*[36]
>
> —Gordon B. Hinkley

From the beginning, the Mormon church has confessed its allegiance to Jesus Christ. Mormon literature emphatically claims to accept and revere the biblical Christ. The publicity booklet *What the Mormons Think of Christ* asserts, "Christ is our Redeemer and our Savior. Except for him there would be no salvation and no redemption, and unless men come unto him and accept him as their Savior, they cannot have eternal life in his presence."[37] "He—Jesus Christ—is the Savior of the world and the Divine Son of God."[38]

In his book *Are Mormons Christians?* written in an attempt to prove that Mormons are Christians, Dr. Stephen Robinson emphasizes continually that Mormons believe in the true, biblical Jesus Christ. In fact, he claims that the evidence that Mormons believe in Jesus Christ is so persuasive that critics have never even dared to raise the issue![39]

The good doctor, apparently, has not read many Christian apologetic works. Evangelical Christian treatments of Mormonism universally maintain that Mormons do not acknowledge the true Jesus Christ. The real issue is not "faith in Christ" but which "Jesus Christ" one believes in. The simple truth is that although Mormons proclaim their belief in the biblical Jesus Christ, like other sects and cults, theirs is a false (even pagan) Christ, one who has nothing to do with the biblical Jesus. As the following chart shows, the Mormon Christ and the biblical Christ are so incompatible that not a single resemblance can be found between them.

Mormon Christ and Christian Christ Incompatibility

THE MORMON JESUS CHRIST	THE BIBLICAL JESUS CHRIST
A created being; the elder brother of Lucifer	Uncreated God
Common (one of many gods) and, in some ways, of minor importance in the *larger* Mormon cosmology	Unique (the Second Person of the *one and only* Godhead) and of supreme importance throughout time, eternity, and all creation
Conceived by a physical sex act between God the Father (Adam or Elohim) and Mary, thus not through a true virgin birth	Conceived by the Holy Spirit, who supernaturally "overshadowed" Mary, thus a true virgin birth
Once sinful and imperfect	Eternally sinless and perfect
Earned his own salvation (exaltation, godhood)	As God, never required salvation
A married polygamist?	An unmarried monogamist

Mormons deny Jesus Christ's unique deity. Mormonism blasphemously teaches that Jesus Christ is a created being by means of sexual intercourse. Mormonism teaches that every person has two births: first, birth as a spirit child in preexistence, and second, much later, birth as a human being. According to Mormon theology, Christ was the first and foremost of subsequent billions of spirit children created through sexual intercourse between the male earth god ("Elohim" or "Adam," of the Garden, depending on early or late Mormonism) and his celestial wife. Later, in order to produce the body for this special spirit child, the earth god again had sexual intercourse, this time with the "virgin" Mary, who then became Jesus' earthly mother.

Jesus Christ is a common God. Mormon teaching implies that Jesus Christ is a "common" God and, in some ways, of minor importance in the larger Mormon cosmology. Mormons do refer to Christ as being "greater" than all other spirit children on earth, but this earth, as discussed previously, is only one of an infinite number of earths, each having their own gods who have existed and evolved for eons longer than Christ. Here on earth, Christ is our "senior" only by achievement and position, *not* by nature or essence.

Christ is also not unique as creator of this earth because Mormonism teaches that Adam, Joseph Smith, and others helped Him to create it. Christ "was aided…by 'many of the noble and great' spirit children of the Father…Adam…Noah…Joseph Smith…."[40]

The nature or essence of Christ is no different from the nature or essence of any spirit child of Elohim, whether of men or of Satan and his demons. Every person on earth has the same nature and essence as Jesus Christ, and He, as they. Although Christ performed better than others in preexistence, He is nevertheless of one nature with all people. Thus, Mormons universally refer to Him as their "elder brother." Again, according to Mormonism, Jesus Christ is not unique in essence but only in achievement and mission. Thus His divinity is not unique, for every exalted person will attain a similar godhood. Neither is His incarnation unique, for all persons are incarnated spirit beings—in preexistence, the offspring of the sexual union of the gods, who then take tabernacles of flesh. Indeed, Christ was only unique in His physical birth; that is, rather than having a human father like the rest of us, His mother had physical sex with the Mormon god "Elohim."

Mormonism teaches that Christ is Satan's brother. In Mormon theology, Jesus Christ is the spirit brother of Satan. Since Satan (and his demons) were also preexistent spirit creations of Elohim and his celestial wife, Satan is Christ's brother as well. In fact, the devil and all demons are the spirit brothers of everyone on earth. Christ, the devil, and all of us are spirit brothers. Jess L. Christensen, director of the LDS Institute of Religion at Utah State University in Logan, Utah, writes in *A Sure Foundation*, "But both the scriptures and the prophets affirm that Jesus Christ and Lucifer are indeed offspring of our Heavenly Father and, therefore, spirit brothers....Jesus was Lucifer's older brother."[41] Another Mormon writer concludes, "As for the devil and his fellow spirits, they are brothers to man and also to Jesus and sons and daughters to God in the same sense that we are."[42]

In light of the above, and many more doctrines, we must be careful not to accept Mormon claims concerning its alleged belief in Christ, or in Christ's biblical uniqueness or deity. Mormons may *claim* to exalt Jesus, for, as McConkie says, "He shall reign to all eternity as King of Kings and Lord of Lords, and God of Gods."[43] But what is often not understood is that literally millions of other people will likewise reign, for as Brigham Young emphasized, all men are "the king of kings and lord of lords in embryo."[44]

Mormonism denies the virgin birth. In his controversial but "divinely inspired" Adam-God discourse of April 9, 1852, Brigham Young taught that the body of Jesus Christ was the product of sexual intercourse between God (Adam) and Mary, who then subsequently married Joseph. But since God (Adam) was also the literal, physical father of Mary (Mary being his literal spirit offspring through celestial intercourse), this amounts to an incestuous and adulterous relationship because, at the same time, she was betrothed in marriage to Joseph. Thus Mary had sexual relations with both her Father in heaven (God Himself) and her spirit brother, Joseph. One apparent effect of this teaching, at least in the minds of some, was to give divine sanction to "spiritual" adultery and even incest, and thus to render the incidents of incestuous polygamy and adultery in Mormon history more acceptable. "After all," they may have reasoned, "God Himself engaged in such practices."[45]

This pagan Mormon teaching denies that Jesus Christ was conceived by the Holy Ghost, and it maintains that Jesus was the literal offspring of the Father because, according to Mormon theology, the Holy Ghost does not have a physical body and therefore could not have had sexual intercourse with Mary. Mormon theology teaches that the Father has a physical body, one "of flesh and bones," so He could easily have had physical sex with Mary to conceive the body of Jesus. Thus, the role of the Holy Spirit in the virgin birth of Jesus Christ, so clearly stated in Matthew 1:18 and Luke 1:35, is rejected by Mormons. The following "inspired" statements by Brigham Young make this clear:

> Now hear it, O inhabitants of the earth, Jew and Gentile, Saint and Sinner! When our Father Adam came into the Garden of Eden, he came into it with a *celestial body,* and brought Eve, *one of his wives,* with him. He helped to make and organize this world. He is MICHAEL, *the Archangel,* THE ANCIENT OF DAYS! about whom holy men have written and spoken—he *is our* Father *and our God, and the only God with whom we have to do.* Every man upon the earth, professing Christians or non-professing, must hear it, and will know it sooner or later....When the Virgin Mary conceived the child Jesus, the Father had begotten him in his own likeness. He was not begotten by the Holy Ghost. And who is the Father? He is the first of the human family [Adam]; and when he took a tabernacle [body], it was begotten by *his Father* in heaven, after the same manner as the tabernacles of Cain, Abel, and the rest of the sons and daughters of Adam and Eve.

> Now remember from this time forth, and forever that *Jesus Christ was not begotten by the Holy Ghost....*"If the son was begotten by the Holy Ghost, it would be very dangerous to baptize and confirm females and give the Holy Ghost to them, lest he should beget children to be palmed upon the Elders by the people, bringing the Elders into great difficulties."[46]

In the *Journal of Discourses* (13:95,264) and the *Millennial Star* (16:543), Young declared this blasphemous doctrine was "the word of the Lord."

In his *Doctrines of Salvation*, the tenth Mormon president and prophet, Joseph Fielding Smith, taught, "Christ was begotten of God. He was not born without the aid of Man and *that Man was God!*"[47] The late LDS theologian Bruce McConkie declared, "Christ was begotten by an Immortal Father in the same way that mortal men are begotten by mortal fathers."[48] The former president and prophet of the Mormon church, Ezra Taft Benson, also believed that Jesus was not conceived by the Holy Ghost: "The body in which he performed his mission in the flesh was sired by that same Holy Being we worship as God, our Eternal Father. Jesus was not the son of Joseph, nor was he begotten by the Holy Ghost. He is the son of the Eternal Father."[49]

Such teachings are hardly biblical (see Matthew 1:18; Luke 1:31-35); instead, they are similar to occult and pagan teachings, which, incidentally, the LDS faith bears resemblance to in other ways. Dr. Anthony Hoekema appropriately concludes, "What these men are saying is that, according to Mormon theology, the body of Jesus Christ was a product of the physical union of God the father and the virgin Mary. One shudders to think of the revolting implications of this view, which brings into what is supposed to be 'Christian' theology one of the most unsavory features of ancient pagan mythology!"[50]

Christ was not eternally sinless. While Mormons staunchly affirm that Christ is sinless, what they mean is that Christ was sinless while on this earth. They do not teach that He was sinless in preexistence.

As we have seen, according to Mormon theology, Jesus was only one of innumerable spirit offspring of the earth god and his celestial wife and, therefore, no different in nature from any other spirit. So He too had to undertake the necessary schooling and progression in the spirit world in order to attain salvation. He had to be tested with good and evil, initially at least, falling into evil like every other spirit son of the earth god. As we documented in our book *What Do Mormons Really Believe?* Mormonism teaches that it is only by direct experience of evil that people learn to choose good.

Bruce McConkie taught that "Christ...is a saved being."[51] The official student manual *Doctrines of the Gospel* instructs students that "the plan of salvation which he [Elohim] designed was to save his children, Christ included; neither Christ nor Lucifer could of themselves save anyone."[52] The same manual also quotes the tenth president and prophet, Joseph Fielding Smith, on the subject:

> The Savior did not have a fullness [of deity] at first, but after he received his body and the resurrection all power was given unto him both in heaven and in earth. Although he was a God, even the Son of God, with power and authority to create this earth and other earths, yet there were some things lacking in which he did not receive until after his resurrection. In other words, he had not received the fullness until he got a resurrected body.[53]

Thus, even though, according to LDS President Benson, "Jesus was a God in the pre-mortal existence," He was still imperfect and lacking certain necessary things.[54] McConkie wrote, "These laws [of salvation], instituted by the father, constitute the gospel of God, which gospel is the plan by which all of his spirit children, Christ included, may gain eternal life."[55] "Jesus Christ is the Son of God....He came to earth to work out his own salvation."[56] "By obedience and devotion to the truth he attained that pinnacle of intelligence which ranked him as a God."[57] A Mormon publicity booklet, *What the Mormons Think of Christ*, asserts, "Christ, the Word, the First Born, had of course, attained unto the status of Godhood while yet in preexistence."[58]

These are but several clear statements showing that Mormon theology unmistakably rejects the Jesus Christ of the Bible. The Mormon Jesus is "another Jesus" (see 2 Corinthians 11:4), who has little if anything to do with true Christian faith. So, again, how can Mormonism be considered a biblical or Christian religion?

16

WHAT DOES MORMONISM TEACH ABOUT SALVATION BY GRACE?

Salvation by grace is one of the glorious doctrines of Christ.
—LDS promotional brochure

We are not saved by grace alone.[59]
—Boyd K. Packer

No biblical doctrine is more important than the doctrine of salvation. Because Mormonism teaches that "there is no salvation outside the Church of Jesus Christ of Latter-day Saints,"[60] its view of salvation is critical, and we need to know what Mormon theology means by it. In the biblical Christian view, salvation is by God's free gift of grace (Ephesians 2:8-9). The Mormon view distorts this in a number of ways. (A much fuller treatment of this issue can be found in our book *What Do Mormons Really Believe?*)

Mormonism vigorously claims that it believes the biblical teaching of salvation by grace. A Mormon promotional brochure declares, "Salvation by grace is one of the glorious doctrines of Christ."[61] In his apologetic text defending the assertion that Mormons are Christians, Dr. Stephen Robinson argues that both the Mormon scriptures and the Mormon church believe that salvation is wholly by grace. Robinson argues, "The charge that Latter-day Saints believe in salvation by works is simply not true. That human beings can save themselves by their own efforts is contrary to the teachings of the Book of Mormon, which eloquently states the doctrine of salvation by grace."[62]

But Dr. Robinson is wrong. The *Book of Mormon* does not state, eloquently or otherwise, the biblical doctrine of salvation by grace. Far from it. In defending his view, the best Dr. Robinson can do is to cite a few weak, if not entirely irrelevant, scriptures from the *Book of Mormon* (Mosiah 2:21,24; 5:7-8; 2 Nephi 2:3-8; 25:23; Alma 5:14-15; Ether 12:27; Moroni 10:32-33). Even the strongest of these passages (2 Nephi 2:3-8) is not considered to teach salvation by grace through faith according to Mormon prophets, presidents, and doctrinal theologians, at least not in any biblical Christian sense. When Mormonism speaks of "salvation by grace," or when it maintains that salvation does not come by "keeping the law," it means something different from what Christians mean by these things.

It is significant that Robinson cites only the *Book of Mormon.* He never cites *Doctrine and Covenants (D&C)*, which is the Mormon scripture that most accurately reflects current Mormon beliefs and from which most Mormon doctrines were originally derived. Robinson forgets to mention that *Doctrines and Covenants* adamantly and repeatedly teaches salvation by works. Further, if Mormonism really teaches salvation by grace, why have Mormon presidents, prophets, theologians, and laypeople staunchly maintained for more than 170 years that salvation is by works? Indeed, one of the few Mormon doctrines that has never been altered, suppressed, or simultaneously affirmed and denied is the doctrine that salvation is by personal merit, by one's own works of righteousness. Mormonism teaches that personal salvation is *never* a free gift secured by grace alone through faith alone as the Bible teaches. Rather, it is secured by individual merit through zealous good works and impeccable law keeping. One thus earns salvation by personal effort and becomes a god in the process. Indeed, the biblical doctrine of salvation by grace through faith alone is one teaching that the Mormon church never has tolerated.[63]

In his *Articles of Faith*, LDS authority James Talmage referred to "a most pernicious doctrine—that of justification by belief alone."[64] "The sectarian [Christian] dogma of justification by faith alone has exercised an influence for evil" and leads to "vicious extremes."[65] Mormon theologian McConkie called it a "soul-destroying doctrine."[66] The tenth president and prophet, Joseph Fielding Smith, emphasized that "mankind [is] damned by [the] 'faith alone' doctrine," and "we must emphatically declare that men must obey these [Gospel] laws if they would be saved."[67] Mormon Apostle Legrand Richards declared, "One erroneous teaching of many Christian churches is: By faith alone we are saved. This false doctrine...would teach man that no matter how great the sin, a confession [of faith in Christ as personal savior] would bring him complete forgiveness and salvation."[68] Early Mormon Apostle Orson Pratt is just as definite:

> Faith alone will not save men; neither will faith and works save them, unless they are [works] of the right kind....True faith and righteous works are essential to salvation; and without both of these no man ever was or ever can be saved....There are some who believe that faith alone, unaccompanied by works, is sufficient for justification, sanctification, and salvation....[They] are without justification— without hope—without everlasting life, and will be damned, the same as unbelievers.[69]

In order to more fully understand Mormon "salvation by grace," we have to see how some key biblical terms surrounding this Mormon doctrine—grace, justification, the new birth, gift, repentance, and sanctification—have been redefined to incorporate works and thus distort the biblical view of salvation as a free gift.

"Grace" incorporates works. When Mormon theologians use the phrase "salvation by grace," they are merely referring to being resurrected from the dead. Beyond that, one's place of residence in

eternity is determined wholly by one's good works. Further, according to Mormonism, salvation by grace is merely an infusing of grace based on good works. This is similar to the Roman Catholic doctrine wherein grace itself becomes a "work," so that as people increase in personal righteousness, more and more "grace" is granted to them. In other words, "grace" is secured from God on the basis of individual merit and personal righteousness. McConkie explains this clearly:

> Grace is granted to men proportionately as they conform to the standards of personal righteousness that are part of the gospel plan.[70]

> Grace, which is an outpouring of the mercy, love, and condescension of God...[is] received—not without works, not without righteousness, not without merit—but by obedience and faith![71]

> Many Protestants...erroneously conclude that men are saved by grace alone without doing the works of righteousness.[72]

"Justification" incorporates works. Biblically, "justification" is the act of God that declares a sinner righteous entirely apart from works, predicated only upon his or her faith in the atoning death of Christ for their sins. In Mormon theology the concept of justification is inextricably bound with conditions of personal merit. According to the Mormon church, justification does not declare one perfectly righteous before God; it only gives one *the opportunity* to earn righteousness before God. Notice McConkie's reformulation: "The very atoning sacrifice itself was wrought out by the Son of God so that men might be justified, that is, so they could *do the things* which will give them eternal life in the celestial realm (*D&C,* 20:21-30, emphasis added)."[73] McConkie also stated, "As with all other doctrines of salvation, justification is available because of the atoning sacrifice of Christ, but it becomes

operative in the life of an individual only on conditions of personal righteousness."[74]

"New birth" incorporates works. President Joseph Fielding Smith taught that "the new birth is also a matter of obedience to law."[75] Smith was echoing the teachings of the *Book of Mormon* (Alma 5:14-30), which declares that to be "born again" a person has to fulfill a number of prerequisites, such as being blameless before God, having an absence of pride and envy. In other words, the new birth is a spiritual *process* secured by good works, not a one-time event secured by faith in Christ. Commenting on this same passage of scripture (about the new birth), McConkie declares that its guidelines enable Mormons "to determine whether and to what extent they have overcome the world, which is the exact extent to which they have in fact been born again."[76]

Biblically, however, being "born again" happens in an instant; it is not a process. Scripture repeatedly refers to the fact that every believer has already been (past tense) born again, without works, simply by faith in Jesus (John 5:24; 6:47; Titus 3:5; 1 Peter 1:3,23).

"Gift" incorporates works. The meaning of the word "gift" is redefined by Mormon theology to mean not something freely given but something that must be earned. The Apostle LeGrand Richards asserted that "to obtain these 'graces,' and the gift of 'eternal salvation,' we must remember that this gift is [given] only to 'all them that obey him.'"[77] McConkie states, "One thing only comes as a free gift to men—the fact of the atoning sacrifice. All other gifts must be earned. That is, God's gifts are bestowed upon those who live the law entitling them to receive whatever is involved."[78]

"Repentance" incorporates works. In Mormonism, the term "repentance" means nothing less than strict obedience to law, rather than the biblical meaning of turning away from one's sins. After a discussion of all the requirements and commandments

that must be fulfilled until the end of one's life in order to achieve salvation, former LDS President Spencer Kimball comments that many people do not understand repentance properly. "They are not 'doing the commandments,' hence they do not repent."[79] Repentance equals obedience. A "transgressor is not fully repentant who neglects his tithing, misses his meetings, breaks the Sabbath, fails in his family prayers, does not sustain the authorities of the Church, breaks the *Word of Wisdom* [church regulations], does not love the Lord nor his fellow man....God cannot forgive unless a transgressor shows a true repentance which spreads to all areas of his life....'Doing the commandments' includes the many activities required of the [Mormon] faithful."[80]

"Sanctification" incorporates works. Similarly, the biblical meaning of sanctification (to be "set apart" to God for His purposes, including growth in holiness) is distorted in Mormon theology. *Doctrines of the Gospel: Student Manual* teaches,

> Members of the Church of Jesus Christ are commanded to become sanctified....*To be sanctified is to become holy and without sin*....Sanctification is attainable because of the atonement of Jesus Christ, but *only if we obey his commandments*....Sanctification is the state of saintliness, a state attained *only by* conformity to the laws and ordinances of the [Mormon] gospel.[81]

Biblically however, sanctification involves three aspects. First, we are (past tense) "set apart" to Christ at the moment of regeneration or saving faith. Second, we are (in the present) progressively being sanctified as we grow in the grace, knowledge, and obedience of our Lord. Third, we are fully sanctified—fully set apart to God and His purposes—when we become glorified and sinless at the moment of our going to be with Him (the future). The first and third of these aspects are entirely by grace, whereas Mormonism makes everything about sanctification a matter of works.

These are but several Mormon redefinitions of biblical meanings. They should be kept in mind in any discussion with individual Mormons.

17

WHAT DOES THE BIBLE TEACH ABOUT SALVATION BY GRACE?

What the Bible teaches about salvation is completely opposed to Mormon doctrine. The Bible clearly reveals that salvation does not come through one's personal righteousness, or personal merit and good works, but only through the grace of God and the individual's faith in Christ's finished work on the Cross.[82] Consider just several passages from the Bible that indicate salvation is by faith, not works:

> I tell you the truth, whoever hears my word and believes him who sent me has eternal life and will not be condemned; he has crossed over from death to life (John 5:24).

> I tell you the truth, he who believes has eternal life (John 6:47).

> Jesus answered and said to them, "This is the work of God, that you believe in Him whom He has sent" (John 6:29 NASB).

> All the prophets testify about him that everyone who believes in him receives forgiveness of sins (Acts 10:43).

> For we maintain that a man is justified by faith apart from observing the law (Romans 3:28).

> ...David also speaks of the blessing upon the man to whom God reckons righteousness apart from works (Romans 4:6 NASB).

> But if it is by grace, it is no longer on the basis of works, otherwise grace is no longer grace (Romans 11:6 NASB).

> For it is by grace you have been saved, through faith—and this not from yourselves, it is the gift of God—not by works, so that no one can boast (Ephesians 2:8-9).

> ...A man is not justified by observing the law, but by faith in Jesus Christ (Galatians 2:16).

> I do not set aside the grace of God, for if righteousness could be gained through the law, Christ died for nothing (Galatians 2:21).
>
> For if a law had been given that could impart life, then righteousness would certainly have come by the law (Galatians 3:21).
>
> All who rely on observing the law are under a curse. ...Clearly no one is justified before God by the law... (Galatians 3:10-11).
>
> He saved us, not on the basis of deeds which we have done in righteousness, but according to His mercy, by the washing of regeneration and renewing by the Holy Spirit (Titus 3:5 NASB).

It is difficult to see how Mormons can continue to maintain that they "believe in the biblical doctrine of salvation by grace through faith," when their scriptures and church teachings are so thoroughly saturated with teaching that salvation comes only by good works. Because of the crucial importance of a true understanding of salvation, the apostle Paul warned everyone clearly: "But even if we or an angel from heaven should preach a gospel other than the one we preached to you, let him be eternally condemned" (Galatians 1:8).

18

What Does Mormonism Teach About the Atonement of Christ?

One frequently finds statements in Mormon literature to the effect that "Christ died for our sins," and Mormonism in general claims to defend the *biblical* teaching on the atonement of Jesus Christ. James Talmage argued that Jesus "bore the weight of the sins of the whole world, not only of Adam but of his posterity."[83] The *Doctrines of the Gospel: Student Manual* emphasizes: "No doctrine in the gospel is more important than the atonement of

Jesus Christ....[The Savior] suffer[ed] for the sins of all the children of God....The infinite atonement affects worlds without number and will save all of God's children except sons of perdition."[84] The *Book of Mormon* also claims that Christ died for our sins. It has Jesus saying, "I...have been slain for the sins of the world" (3 Nephi 11:14). And it teaches that "the sufferings and death of Christ atone for their [people's] sins, through faith and repentance" (Alma 22:14).

While these statements generally sound Christian, Mormons mean something quite different by them, just as they do with the terms surrounding the Trinity, salvation, and other doctrines. Mormons, in fact, do not believe that Christ has *effectively* died for their sins and paid the actual penalty of divine justice necessary for their complete and eternal forgiveness through faith in Christ. Further, Mormons believe that forgiveness of sins is not immediately received upon true faith and repentance. True forgiveness, for them, requires a lengthy probationary period, and serious sins will cause the loss of salvation. Thus Mormon "salvation," and by implication Christ's atonement, does not cover forgiveness of "serious sins."[85]

Consistent with a works-view of salvation, in Mormon theology the atonement includes human obedience, especially to laws and commandments. President Benson taught that the atonement of Christ's death is effective for "redeeming all of us from physical death, and redeeming those of us from spiritual death *who will obey the laws and ordinances of the gospel*."[86] The *Doctrines of the Gospel* claims that Jesus came to save only those who would obey Him, because mercy is extended only to those who keep God's commandments. "If we do not keep God's commandments, we must suffer for our own sins."[87] The Mormon text *A Sure Foundation* states: "We believe that it is Christ's atonement that saves us but that we must endure to the end in doing good works *if his atonement is to take effect on our behalf*....It is by the atonement of Christ that we are saved, but *it is necessary that we keep the commandments* and obey the ordinances God has given us."[88] In essence, although without Christ's atonement salvation would not be possible, salvation itself is the reward for individual merit. Thus point 3 of the Articles of Faith of Joseph Smith states, "We believe that through the atonement of Christ, all mankind may be saved, by obedience to the laws and ordinances of the gospel."

Ideas like these explain why Mormon discussions of the atonement are noticeable for their lack of affirming actual forgiveness of sins through Christ's death alone. It also explains, to a large degree, why Mormons do not know the true Gospel, for they have never heard it within Mormonism. One former 20-year Mormon (who taught doctrine in the church) said that he never once heard that Christ actually (effectively) died on the cross for his sin. This is not unique within Mormonism; it is characteristic.[89]

In essence Mormonism teaches that the atonement provides the *opportunity to earn salvation* through personal merit. Just as a college degree does not actually secure a job and salary, but only makes earning them possible, so Christ's death does not actually secure salvation and glorification (exaltation) but only makes earning them possible by good works. In fact, even if all the faith in the world were placed in Christ's death, this still would not forgive a single sin apart from law-keeping. In Mormonism, then, the substitutionary, saving value of Christ's atonement is nonexistent. Their theology denies that Christ's death paid the full penalty for our sins, resulting in complete forgiveness at the moment of faith (see 1 Corinthians 15:3; Colossians 2:13; Hebrews 9:12). Dr. McMurrin sums up the Mormon distortion on the atonement clearly:

> Mormon theology has with considerable ingenuity constructed its doctrine of salvation around the fall and the atonement, but with radically unorthodox meanings.... The meaning of the grace of God given through the atonement of Christ is that man by his freedom can now merit salvation....But that Christ has taken the sins of the world upon himself does not mean, in Mormon theology, that he has by his sinless sacrifice brought the free gift of salvation

to mortals steeped in original and actual sin and therefore unworthy of the grace bestowed upon them. In the Mormon doctrine, Christ redeems men from the physical and spiritual death imposed upon them by the transgression of Adam....But he does not in any way absolve them of the consequences of their own actual evil or save them with high glory in the absence of genuine merit.[90]

19

IS MORMONISM AN OCCULT RELIGION?

To this point we have seen that the LDS faith, whatever else it is, is not biblical faith. But there is one more concern that must be addressed in this section. The Bible is very clear that true Christians are to avoid occult practices. It is unthinkable that the founder of any Christian church would also be a practitioner of the occult arts. Consider a few scriptures that speak to this:

> Let no one be found among you who...practices divination or sorcery, interprets omens, engages in witchcraft, or casts spells, or who is a medium or spiritist or who consults the dead. Anyone who does these things is detestable to the LORD... (Deuteronomy 18:10-12).

> He [King Manasseh] did evil in the eyes of the LORD....He bowed down to all the starry hosts and worshiped them.... [He] practiced sorcery, divination and witchcraft, and consulted mediums and spiritists (2 Chronicles 33:2-3,6).

> They consult a wooden idol and are answered by a stick of wood. A spirit of prostitution leads them astray; they are unfaithful to their God (Hosea 4:12).

> Many of those who believed now came and openly confessed their evil deeds. A number who had practiced sorcery brought their scrolls together and burned them publicly (Acts 19:18-19).

In no uncertain terms, the Bible condemns sorcery, magic, astrology, spiritism, divination, dowsing and so on as trafficking with the powers of darkness, but these are precisely the kinds of things practiced by Joseph Smith. The early LDS connections to the occult can be seen in detail in works such as *Early Mormonism and the Magical Worldview* (Signature Books) by noted historian D. Michael Quinn; *The Refiner's Fire: The Making of Mormon Cosmology, 1644–1844* (Cambridge University Press) by John L. Brooke; and Lance S. Owen's "Joseph Smith and the Kabbalah: The Occult Connection" (*Dialogue,* vol. 27, no. 3, 1994), which received the Mormon Historical Association "Best Article of the Year" award for 1995.

Again we come to one of those points that many Mormons, being uninformed, will find hard to accept about their religion—its occult dimension. But the facts are clear. From Joseph Smith onward, numerous Mormon leaders and prophets have had strong occult interests. For example, the Smith family was very interested in the occult practice of astrology.[91] This is not the accusation of "enemies" of the Mormon church but of perhaps its then most academically qualified, but now excommunicated historian, the just mentioned Dr. D. Michael Quinn, who holds a Ph.D. in History from Yale University:

> Astrology was important to members of the Smith family....Brigham Young stated in 1861 that "an effort was made in the days of Joseph to establish astrology."...The Hyrum Smith family preserved a magic dagger inscribed with Mars, the ruling planet of Joseph Smith Sr.'s birth year. The Hyrum Smith family also possessed magic parchments inscribed with the astrological symbols of the planets and the Zodiac...and the Emma Smith Badamon family preserved a magic artifact consecrated to Jupiter, the ruling planet of Joseph Smith Jr.'s birth. Based on interviews in 1886 with disaffected Mormons of early Church membership, one anti-Mormon wrote, "The only thing the

> Prophet believed in was astrology. This is a fact generally known to old 'Nauvoo Mormons.'"[92]

The Smith family also practiced ritual magic, used divining rods, and employed crystal gazing. Dr. Quinn observes,

> The Smiths left direct evidence of their practice of ritual magic. In addition to the magic dagger, among Hyrum Smith's possessions at his death were three parchments—lamens, in occult terms—inscribed with signs and names of ceremonial magic....Palmyra neighbors reported that Joseph Smith Sr. and Joseph Smith Jr. were drawing magic circles in the mid-1820's....Several sources indicate that Joseph Jr. engaged in folk magic activities during the summers of the 1820's away from Palmyra, often in Pennsylvania.[93]

> He was a part-time but active participant in folk magic, using divining rods and "seer stones," or "peep-stones," to find buried treasure. Both father and son, from about 1819, were active in such treasure-digging." (See www.irr.org.)

From the perspective of occult revelation, Smith's dependence upon magic ritual and other forms of the dark arts makes the occult origin of the *Book of Mormon* more credible. As we saw, Smith regularly participated in the occult practice of crystal gazing, using "peep stones," or seer stones to receive psychic information. He would place these stones in a hat, bury his face in the hat, and then "see" visions of buried treasure, lost property, and suchlike.[94] Of course, according to witnesses, this was also how the *Book of Mormon* was translated. (See "Section II: The Book of Mormon.")

The occult origin of the Mormon religion therefore seems to involve more than just the "distorted reasoning of church enemies." Smith's dependence upon the supernatural for his new religion is clear, and he was in many ways indistinguishable from a spiritist medium—as lectures of the time by church leaders like Parley Pratt reveal (see *Journal of Discourses*, 2:44-46; 1:12-15). Thus, 1) the *Book of Mormon* was an occultly derived text;

2) *Doctrine and Covenants* was an occultly derived text containing more than 100 spiritistic revelations; 3) *The Pearl of Great Price* was an occultly derived text, being another translation done by occult power; and 4) Smith's own revision of the King James Bible, his "inspired translation," may also have been accomplished by occult means.

Occult influence in Mormonism is also seen in the second president of the church, Brigham Young, who to some degree held a mediumistic philosophy. This can be seen in his conviction that many of the dead are schooled in the afterlife before being permitted an opportunity to progress spiritually:

> If a person is baptized for the remission of sins, and dies a short time thereafter, he is not prepared at once to enjoy a fullness of the glory promised to the faithful in the Gospel; for he must be schooled while in the spirit, and other departments of the house of God, passing on from truth to truth, from intelligence to intelligence, until he is prepared to again receive his body and to enter into the presence of the Father and the Son. We cannot enter into celestial glory in our present state of ignorance and mental darkness.... We have more friends behind the veil than on this side, and they hail us more joyfully than you were welcomed by your parents and friends in this world; and you will rejoice more when you meet them than you ever rejoiced to see a friend in this life.[95]

This mediumistic teaching is endorsed in later Mormonism. A previous president and prophet of the Mormon church, Spencer W. Kimball, taught,

> It is the destiny of the spirits of men to come to this earth and travel a [spiritual] journey of indeterminate length.... While we lack recollection of our pre-mortal life, before coming to this earth all of us understood definitely the purpose of our being here....We understood also that after a period varying from seconds to decades of mortal life we would die, our bodies would go back to Mother Earth

> from which they had been created, and our spirits would go to the spirit world, where we would further train for our eternal destiny. After a period, there would be a resurrection or a reunion of the body and the spirit, which would render us immortal and make possible our further climb toward perfection and godhood.[96]

Sounding like a typical New Age channeler today, Kimball said, "Men came to earth consciously to obtain their schooling, their training and development, and to perfect themselves."[97]

Mormon theologian Duane S. Crowther has stated various (unbiblical) guidelines by which Mormons can contact spirits and feel safe about it. He also explained that according to Mormon belief there are at least five categories of spirits who can minister to Mormons and others. There are "pre-mortal spirits," "translated beings," "righteous spirits," "evil spirits," and "resurrected beings." The fact that Mormonism offers so many opportunities for contact with the spirits is one reason why Mormonism can properly be classified as a spiritistic religion. Crowther himself defines one of these categories in characteristically mediumistic terms: "righteous spirits return to earth to: give counsel, give comfort, obtain or give information, serve as guardian angels, prepare us for death, summon mortals into the spirit world, escort the dying through the veil of death."[98]

Joseph F. Smith, the sixth president and prophet of the Mormon church, also supported necromancy—spiritistic and mediumistic contacts with the dead:

> Our fathers and mothers, brothers, sisters and friends who have passed away from this earth, having been faithful... may have a mission given them to visit their relatives and friends upon the earth again, bringing from the divine Presence messages of love, of warning, or reproof and instruction, to those whom they had learned to love in the flesh....Joseph Smith, Hyrum Smith, Brigham Young, Heber C. Kimball, Jed M. Grant, David Patten, Joseph Smith, Sen., and all those noble men who took an active

> part in the establishment of this work, and who died true and faithful to their trust, have the right and privilege, and possess the keys and power, to minister to the people of God in the flesh who live now....These are correct principles. There is no question about that in my mind. It is according to the scripture; it is according to the revelation of God to the Prophet Joseph Smith; and it is a subject upon which we may dwell with pleasure and perhaps profit to ourselves, provided we have the Spirit of God to direct us.[99]

The fourth Mormon president and prophet, Wilford Woodruff, stated in 1880:

> After the death of Joseph Smith I saw and conversed with him many times in my dreams in the night season....I have had many interviews with brother Joseph until the last fifteen or twenty years of my life....I had many interviews with President Young, and with Heber C. Kimball, and Geo. A. Smith, and Jedediah M. Grant, and many others who are dead. *They attended our conference, they attended our meetings.*[100]

This is just the tip of a vast iceberg. The extent of occult practice throughout Mormon history until the present is significant. [We presented a brief summary in our *Behind the Mask of Mormonism* (chapters 18-20).] Even in LDS practice today we find occult practices under another name, especially in association with the temple ceremonies. For example, former president Ezra Taft Benson declared that the spirits of the dead actively assist Mormons: "Visitors, seen and unseen, from the world beyond, are often close to us....Sometimes actions here, by the priesthood of God, the First Presidency and the Twelve, as we meet in the Temple, have been planned and influenced by leaders of the priesthood on the other side [the spirit world]. I am sure of that. We have evidence of it....These righteous spirits are close by us."[101]

Even though the Bible condemns all forms of occultism, including the not infrequent LDS practices of necromancy and spirit contact, everything from automatic writing to out-of-body excursions and other occult practices has been endorsed by Mormons.[102] Mormons who believe that this is acceptable with God have, to varying degrees, adopted occultism in the guise of divine pursuits. One can but wonder, how many well-meaning Mormons have been ensnared in occult practices outside their church because they were conditioned to accept occultism within the church?

SECTION V

A CRITIQUE OF THE LDS CLAIM TO BE CHRISTIAN

Mormons are Christians precisely because they sincerely say they are. No other criterion is needed. . . ."[1]

—Daniel C. Petersen and Stephen D. Ricks

But for Evangelicals to say that "because we don't believe in Jesus 'correctly,' that we don't believe in him at all" seems to me egocentric. We don't need their permission to believe in Jesus. If they think we do, then to hell with them."[2]

—Dr. Stephen Robinson

The Church of Jesus Christ of Latter-day Saints is Christian but is neither Catholic nor Protestant. Rather, it is a restoration of the original church established by Jesus Christ.[3]

20

IS THE MORMON CLAIM TO BE CHRISTIAN AN UNINTENTIONAL MISINFORMING?

We have so far documented two things: 1) that the LDS claim to be the true, restored Church of Jesus Christ is wrong because the evidence offered in substantiation is spurious, and 2) that Mormon teaching is actively opposed to the teachings of the Bible and Christianity in many vital areas, including the nature of God, Jesus Christ, salvation, man, the atonement, and the occult.

In spite of this, the LDS faithful maintain they are the only true Christians. In this section we will briefly address three key issues: 1) the reason for Mormonism's claim to be a Christian religion; 2) what various authorities have said about Mormonism being a Christian religion; 3) Mormonism's true beliefs about Christianity.[4]

Put simply, Mormons claim they are Christian because they "believe in Jesus" and "believe in Christian and biblical teachings" such as the Trinity, salvation by grace, the atonement, the Bible, and so on. However, as should be plain by now, the real problem is not established Christian doctrine, rather it is the LDS Church's ersatz redefining and distortion of Christian doctrine that leads to the confusion of the public at large, Mormons in general, and even many Christians. Former Mormons Jerald and Sandra Tanner, who have diligently sought to help both Mormons and Christians understand what Mormonism really teaches and why it can't be considered Christian, tell us that the greatest problem the Christian church faces concerning Mormonism is that far too many Christians think Mormonism *is* a Christian religion.

Unfortunately, as far as Mormons are concerned, the only way this error in thinking can be maintained is by refusing to seriously examine what the Bible *actually* teaches—for example, by assuming that the LDS authorities have got it right when they claim to represent true Christianity and state that historic Christianity is a false religion. But this is a potentially fatal assumption. Until individual Mormons carefully study the Bible independently and critically evaluate the evidence for their own religion, they will continue to be led astray by a church leadership that, historically, has cared very little for the truth.

Both Mormons and Christians will agree that all of us are responsible for what we do in life, and that no one will escape a final accounting. It is clearly true that many Mormons are victims of the betrayal of LDS leadership (just as some Christians are in churches that have bad leadership), but this does not absolve anyone from the personal responsibility of loving God, knowing basic Bible doctrine, and proclaiming the truth.

Is the Mormon claim to be Christian an unintentional misinforming? Are Mormons innocently deceived in their claim to be Christian, or do they know they are not Christian and make the claim for purposes of proselytizing Christianity? First, there is little doubt that most Mormons honestly believe they are Christian. They accept what the LDS leadership and Mormon scriptures have declared as to the alleged apostasy of Christianity and its restoration through Joseph Smith without investigating the matter further. It is very regrettable that most LDS do not seek to independently and objectively confirm the claims of their faith, but that is the choice that has been made by millions. However, many LDS scholars and many of those who control the church cannot be considered innocent victims of someone else's distortions. They are familiar with historic Christianity, and they have been confronted with the evidence against the LDS faith but choose not to accept it and claim to be Christian anyway.

Some LDS scholars go further and deceptively attempt to rewrite history or even scripture to make the LDS faith "Christian." In this they are sadly following their own prophets. For example, in his "inspired version" of the Bible, Joseph Smith clearly distorts scripture to support LDS doctrine; for example, in Romans 4:5, the word "not" is inserted into the biblical verse ("...who justifies NOT the ungodly") in order to deny the biblical teaching on justification by faith. Modern LDS Bible commentators such as Bruce McConkie in his *Doctrinal New Testament Commentary* cite Smith's mistranslation to prove that "God will *not* justify the ungodly," the exact *opposite* of what Romans 4:5 teaches. Indeed, despite the fact that Smith declared he produced his translation under the same divine inspiration claimed for the LDS scriptures, the Utah church does not accept it fully because it contains doctrines that contradict those of the modern church. In other words, as it does with the Bible generally, it picks and chooses what it will or will not accept, even from its own scriptures (for example, the *D&C* teaching in chapter 132 on polygamy being an eternal covenant that must be obeyed upon pain of damnation). Regardless, there are many Mormon scholars who know the LDS claim to being Christian is unsubstantiated. They just don't like it, they want to be seen as Christian, and they conveniently ignore or distort the facts.

What does it mean to be a Christian? To be a Christian is to be a committed follower of the *biblical* Jesus Christ, which logically includes believing in the Bible as He did—as God's inerrant Word (John 17:17)—and in the doctrines of historic Christianity logically derived from God's Word. This is why the *Oxford American Dictionary* defines "Christian" as "of the doctrines of Christianity, believing in or based on these." "Christianity" is defined as "the religion based on the belief that Christ was the incarnate Son of God and on his teachings."[5]

A true Christian is one who has personally received the biblical Jesus Christ as his or her Lord and Savior and who leads a lifestyle in concert with orthodox biblical teaching. It involves a loving and committed relationship with the God of the Bible—not merely going to church on Sundays, believing in Jesus in an intellectual sense, or attempting to live "a Christian life." It is certainly not claiming to be a Christian while simultaneously rejecting all major Christian doctrines in support of an occult religion. Being a true Christian incorporates adherence to accurate doctrine and a godly lifestyle centered on a personal relationship with the living Jesus Christ.

In spite of this, the Mormon church deliberately seeks to be known as a Christian religion. President Ezra Taft Benson answered a resounding "yes" to the question, "*Are Mormons Christians?*"[6] Jack Weyland, a physics professor at BYU Idaho and a former bishop in a South Dakota stake, mentions that several times he has faced the situation where someone has told him or another Mormon that they are not Christian: "And every time it happens I'm astonished. I usually respond by saying, 'but the name of the church is the Church of Jesus Christ of Latter-day Saints. Every prayer we utter is offered in his name. Every ordinance we perform we do in his name. We believe all the Bible says about him....'"[7] Dr. Harold Goodman, a Brigham Young University professor and Latter-day Saints mission president argues, "Anyone that believes in Christ is a Christian. And we believe that we are Christians."[8]

Perhaps the most comprehensive defense of the idea that the Mormon religion is Christian is found in Stephen Robinson's *Are Mormons Christians?* Robinson, who received a Ph.D. in biblical studies from Duke University,[9] agrees that the charge that Mormons are not Christians "is often the most commonly heard criticism of the LDS Church and its doctrines."[10] And he allows that this "is a serious charge indeed."[11] However, he argues,

> Most of the time the charge that the Latter-day Saints are not Christians has absolutely nothing to do with LDS belief or non-belief in Jesus Christ, or with LDS acceptance or rejection of the New Testament as the word of God. If the term *Christian* is used, as it is in standard English to mean someone who accepts Jesus Christ as the Son of God and the Savior of the world, then the charge that Mormons aren't Christians is false.[12]

But in characteristic LDS fashion, Robinson discards the evidence he does not like and drags red herrings over the historical and theological landscape. As Robert B. Stewart, Ph.D., assistant professor of philosophy and theology at New Orleans Baptist Theological Seminary wrote in a review, "Like a good lawyer, Robinson realizes that if his case cannot be made on the basis of the evidence, he must do all he can to keep the evidence out of court." "...Robinson intentionally diverts the reader's attention from the truly significant issues...."[13]

Dr. Robinson, despite his effort, freely concedes that Mormonism 1) rejects traditional Christian orthodoxy;[14] 2) rejects the historic orthodox view of the Trinity;[15] and 3) rejects the specific orthodox Christian teaching concerning God.[16] So one wonders, given the demonstrated unity of Christian scripture and the historic creeds, how can the LDS faith possibly be considered Christian? How can Robinson express astonishment when someone argues Mormonism should not be considered Christian?

It is not logically possible that a religion which rejects the biblical Trinity and accepts polytheism, which denies that God always existed and instead maintains that God was once a man who evolved into godhood, which teaches works-salvation and denies salvation by grace, which offers a pagan view of the virgin birth, which endorses the occult, and so on, can legitimately call itself Christian. Mormonism is not true Christianity, and true Mormons cannot be considered Christians.[17]

For Mormons to maintain they are truly Christian they must ignore the weight of 20 centuries of history and the conclusions of most people outside the church who have seriously and independently investigated the issue.

21

WHAT HAVE OTHERS SAID ABOUT MORMONISM BEING A CHRISTIAN RELIGION?

Because there is such widespread misunderstanding concerning the religious status of the Mormon church, we will document numerous declarations by various church bodies and reputable religious scholars and authorities, Christian and non-Christian, who classify Mormonism as a non-Christian religion.

1. The United Methodist Church concluded at their General Conference, May 2-12, 2000: "The church of Jesus Christ of Latter-day Saints, by self-definition, does not fit within the bounds of the historic, apostolic tradition of Christian faith."[18]

2. The Presbyterian Church (USA): "...Mormonism is a new and emerging religious tradition distinct from the historic apostolic tradition of the Christian Church.... Latter-day Saints

and the historic churches view the canon of scriptures and interpret shared scriptures in radically different ways. They use the same words with dissimilar meanings."[19]

3. The Southern Baptist Convention, North American Mission Board: "The Church of Jesus Christ of Latter-Day Saints (LDS or Mormon church) professes to be a Christian church. However, a careful comparison of basic doctrinal positions of that church to those of historical, biblical Christianity reveal many radical differences."[20]

4. As far as we know, even the liberal World Council of Churches refuses to classify Mormonism as a Christian religion.[21]

5. In his book *The Theological Foundations of the Mormon Religion*, LDS scholar Sterling M. McMurrin, E.E. Ericksen Distinguished Professor, professor of History, professor of Philosophy of Education, and dean of the Graduate School at the University of Utah, sets as a purpose: "facilitating understanding of Mormonism."[22] Noting that Mormon theology has "a radically unorthodox concept of God," he observed that "in its conception of God as in its doctrine of man, Mormonism is a radical departure from the established theology, both Catholic and Protestant."[23]

6. In his book *Is Mormonism Christian?* Gordon Fraser, author of four books on Mormonism, comments, "We object to Mormon missionaries posing as Christians, and our objections are based on the differences between what they are taught by their General Authorities and what the Bible teaches."[24]

7. In *The Maze of Mormonism*, the late Dr. Walter Martin, an acknowledged authority on comparative religion and biblical theology, observed, "In no uncertain terms, the Bible condemns the teachings of the Mormon Church."[25]

8. Former Mormons Jerald and Sandra Tanner, who have done perhaps more in-depth research into Mormonism than

anyone else, write in *The Changing World of Mormonism*, "The Mormon Church is certainly not built upon the teachings of the Bible....Mormonism...is not even based on the Book of Mormon."[26]

9. In his book *The Four Major Cults*, theologian Dr. Anthony Hoekema emphasizes, "We must at this point assert, in the strongest possible terms, that Mormonism does not deserve to be called a Christian religion. It is basically anti-Christian and anti-biblical."[27]

10. The *Evangelical Dictionary of Theology* concludes that the Mormon attempt to be Christian "does little justice to either Mormon theology or the Christian tradition."[28]

11. The *Encyclopedia Britannica* concludes: "Mormon doctrine diverges from the orthodoxy of established Christianity, particularly in its polytheism, in affirming that God has evolved from man and that men might evolve into gods, that the Persons of the Trinity are distinct beings, and that men's souls have preexisted."[29]

12. *The New Schaff-Herzog Encyclopedia of Religious Knowledge* comments,

> So far as the Bible is concerned, Joseph Smith and his successors have taken such liberties with its meaning, and even with its text, that it cannot be said to have any authority for a Mormon....Its doctrine of God, for example, is widely different from that of the Christian Church. The Mormon conception of deity rather resembles that of Buddhism. From it a system of anthropomorphisms has been developed, which far exceeds that of any Christian sect in any age....[30]

13. *The New International Dictionary of the Christian Church* concludes, "An examination of the doctrines taught by the Mormon Church will reveal that they deny most of the cardinal teachings of the Christian faith."[31]

14. Countless theologians and biblical scholars agree that Mormonism is not Christian. For example, Robert B. Stewart, Ph.D., assistant professor of Philosophy and Theology, New Orleans Baptist Theological Seminary says: "Mormonism cannot be accepted as Christian. There are irreconcilable differences between Mormonism and Christianity concerning the nature of Scripture, God, and Jesus Christ. The apparent similarities between the two systems quickly fade when LDS terminology is properly interpreted."[32]

    Professor of New Testament Craig L. Blomberg, author of an earlier work that received a fair amount of criticism for "muddying the waters," *How Wide the Divide? A Mormon and Evangelical in Conversation* (which did not address the specific issue of whether LDS were Christian), concluded in 2002: "The real problem from an evangelical perspective—or any orthodox Christian perspective—is to find a *meaningful* way to include Mormonism within Christianity. I cannot, as of this writing, therefore, affirm with integrity that either Mormonism as a whole or any individual, based solely on his or her affirmation of the totality of LDS doctrine, deserves the label 'Christian' in any standard or helpful sense of the word."[33]

In conclusion, for Mormons to argue the LDS faith is Christian, let alone the only true Christianity, is tantamount to a denial of two millennia of history and shutting down departments of biblical studies and historic and systematic theology everywhere.

22

WHAT ARE THE REAL MORMON BELIEFS ABOUT CHRISTIANITY?

In closing this section we thought it might be helpful to cite some of the true views of Christianity that are held by the Mormon church. Because some of these are in the background of

Mormonism, people may find them surprising, being so far different as they are from the neighborly image the church seeks to uphold. Because we will be quoting LDS presidents and prophets it is important to understand the divine authority they claim to have. LDS leaders have emphasized that each president and prophet of the church gives "living scripture" and speaks with "the authority of God...[as] the mouthpiece for God," and that "nothing a Mormon President says can be incorrect."[34] The "Core beliefs and Doctrines" listed at www.lds.org observes, "Divine revelation for the direction of the entire Church comes from God to the president of the Church, who is viewed by Latter-day Saints as a prophet in the same sense as are Abraham, Moses, Peter and other biblical leaders."[35]

President Ezra Taft Benson, in his well-known February 26, 1980, speech, "Fourteen Fundamentals in Following the Prophet" (widely available online), quoting *D&C*, 21:4-6, emphasized, "We are to 'give heed unto all his words'—as if from the Lord's 'own mouth.' "[36] Here are a few of his "fundamentals":

> 1. The prophet is the only man who speaks for the Lord in everything.
>
> 2. The living prophet is more vital to us than the standard works.
>
> 4. The prophet will never lead the Church astray.
>
> 6. The prophet does not have to say "thus saith the Lord" to give us scripture.
>
> 14. The prophet and the presidency—the living prophet and the first presidency—follow them and be blessed—reject them and suffer.

Thus, when we quote what the LDS presidents say about Christianity or Christians, we are citing true LDS beliefs. Here is what several presidents and prophets of the church, as well as other LDS authorities, have said.

Christians are unbelievers. Second president and prophet Brigham Young dogmatically insisted that "Christians profess to believe in Jesus Christ; but, if be told the truth, not one of them really believes in him."[37] In the introduction to Joseph Smith's *History of the Church*, leading Mormon church historian Brigham Henry Roberts (1857–1933) declared that those who profess belief in the great defining creeds of Christianity (Nicean, Athanasian, and so on) "are wandering in the darkness of the mysticisms of the old pagan philosophies."[38] He further claims that these creeds "exhibit the wide departure—the absolute apostasy—that has taken place in respect of this most fundamental of all doctrines of religion—the doctrine of God. Truly, 'Christians' have denied the Lord that bought them, and turned literally to fables."[39]

Christians are satanic false teachers. First president and prophet Joseph Smith, who still remains the most influential man in Mormonism, said that Christian pastors "are of their father the devil....We shall see all the priests who adhere to the sectarian [Christian] religions of the day, with all their followers, without one exception, receive their portion with the devil and his angels."[40]

In 1 Nephi chapters 13–14 and elsewhere, the *Book of Mormon* calls the Christian church "a church which is most abominable above all other churches"; it is "the great and abominable church" founded by the devil; it is "the mother of abominations" and the great "whore of Babylon," and the "whore of all the earth."[41] In an official compilation of Joseph Smith's writings, *Teachings of the Prophet Joseph Smith*, we find the following assessment: "What is it that inspires professors of Christianity generally with the hope of salvation? It is that smooth, sophisticated influence of the devil, by which he deceives the whole world."[42]

Christians are ignorant of the things of God. President and prophet Brigham Young declared:

> With regard to true theology, a more ignorant people never lived than the present so-called Christian world.[43]

> The Christian world, so called, are heathens as to their knowledge of the salvation of God.[44]

> The Christian world, I discovered...was groveling in darkness.[45]

> We may very properly say that the sectarian [Christian] world [does] not know anything correctly, so far as pertains to salvation....They are more ignorant than children.[46]

The third president and prophet of the church, John Taylor, held the same view:

> We talk about Christianity, but it is a perfect pack of nonsense....And the Devil could not invent a better engine to spread his work than the Christianity of the 19th century.[47]

> I consider that if I ever lost any time in my life, it was while studying the Christian theology. Sectarian [Christian] theology is the greatest tomfoolery in the world.[48]

> What does the Christian world know about God? Nothing; yet these very men assume the right and power to tell others what they shall and what they shall not believe in. Why, so far as the things of God are concerned, they are the veriest fools, they know neither God nor the things of God.[49]

> What! Are Christians ignorant? Yes, as ignorant of the things of God as the brute beast.[50]

Mormon Apostle Orson Pratt declared that "the whole of Christendom is as destitute of Bible Christianity as the idolatrist Pagans."[51] B.H. Roberts, noted Mormon church historian and member of the "First Council of Seventy," referred to Christians as those "who are blindly led by the blind."[52]

Christians teach false doctrines. Mormon Apostle Orson Pratt also emphasized the evils of Christianity:

> Will Christendom have the unblushing impudence to call themselves the people of God...? How long will the heavens suffer such wickedness to go unpunished![53]

> Another evil of no small magnitude is the vast amount of false doctrines which are taught, and extensively believed, and practiced throughout Christendom. Doctrines which are calculated to ruin the soul....These soul-destroying doctrines...are taught in Christendom, and...millions have had the wickedness to believe [them]....Now what will become of all these false teachers...and what will become of the people who suffer themselves to be led by such hypocrites? They will, every soul of them, unless they repent of these false doctrines, be cast down to hell....Such heaven-daring wickedness is calculated to sink these vile impostors to the lowest hell. And unless the people repent of having received baptism and other ordinances of the Gospel at the hands of such deceivers...[and] embrace the fulness of the Gospel which God has revealed anew in the *Book of Mormon*...[every one] of you will, most assuredly, be damned.[54]

In our time the rhetoric is somewhat toned down but the reproachful view remains. President and prophet Joseph Fielding Smith stated that "gospel truth [was] perverted and defiled" by Catholicism until it became a pagan abomination, and even the Reformation "perpetuated these evils and, therefore, the same corrupted doctrines and practices were perpetuated in these Protestant organizations."[55]

In his *Mormon Doctrine*, LDS theologian Bruce McConkie universally condemns all non-Mormon churches, asserting that "a perverted Christianity holds sway among the so-called Christians of apostate Christendom."[56] He also observes, commenting on the *Book of Mormon* (1 Nephi, chapters 13–14; 2 Nephi, chapters 28–29): "The Church of the Devil and the Great and Abominable Church are [terms] used to identify all churches or organizations of whatever name or nature...which are designed to take men on a course that leads away from God and his laws and thus from salvation in the kingdom of God [the Mormon Church]....There is no salvation outside this one true Church, the [Mormon] Church of Jesus Christ."[57] In his *Doctrinal New Testament Commentary*,

McConkie alleges that Christians are the true enemies of God because the true teachings of God "have been changed and perverted by an apostate Christendom."[58] Further, modern Christians are ignorant of God's true purposes,[59] and Christian doctrines are the "doctrines of devils."[60] Thus, the Christian church is part of "the great and abominable church" of the devil preparing men "to be damned."[61]

One can only conclude that despite the claims of the Mormon church and the sincere conviction of many Mormon people, Mormonism is not a Christian religion. From its inception, Mormonism has distanced itself from historic Christian faith, believing that Christianity is an apostate religion that damns the souls of its followers.

23

WHAT ARE SOME HELPS ON TALKING WITH MORMONS?

As Christian editor Paul Gossard noted, "What is needed most to help Mormons is a sacrificial willingness to make friends with them and present the true Jesus to them." Many Christians are doing just this—so much so that the LDS church has taken note of the drain and responded with countermeasures.

As is true for most other allegedly Christian groups, talking with Mormons can be difficult because of the semantics barrier. When Christian or biblical words are used, they have a meaning unique to the group, not one consistent with historic Christian or biblical meaning. Both Mormons and Christians need to understand that when they use terms such as God, Jesus Christ, trinity, grace, virgin birth, salvation, heaven, hell, the scriptures, and so on, they will be talking past one another unless they understand what each group means by these terms (see Doctrinal Summary).

Christians who never discover what Mormons mean by these terms may assume they are talking with other Christians.

In addition, the fact that most Mormons are uninformed on their doctrinal history compounds the problem. A common response to the discussion of the specifics of Mormon teaching historically is, "We do not believe that." Whether they do or don't, in giving this response, they deny the teachings of their own inspired prophets. (See Question 28.)

At the very least, Mormons can be informed that their definitions of key theological terms, such as God, Jesus Christ, and salvation, do not conform to historic or biblical meanings. The burden of proof remains with the LDS to give some evidence for their definitions of words and theological beliefs. So far, none has been provided.

One of the most important issues to discuss with Mormons is the issue of spiritual authority. For example, Joseph Smith's false prophecies clearly prove that he was not a true prophet of God. Because he spoke in the name of the Lord and gave false prophecies, the only option available is to consider him a false prophet. We earlier quoted Smith's own words to this effect. God tells us the true prophet is "recognized as one truly sent by the Lord *only* if his prediction comes true" (Jeremiah 28:9, emphasis added). This is because "whatever I say *will* be fulfilled, declares the sovereign LORD" (Ezekiel 12:28, emphasis added). God's accuracy will be nothing less than 100 percent, for He is a God "who does not lie" (Titus 1:2); indeed lying is impossible for Him (Hebrews 6:18; cf. 1 John 2:21).

Coupled with visual documentation of Smith's false prophecies cited in this book (or others if necessary, see www.utlm.org), the following verses may be useful in discussion:

> You may say to yourselves, "How can we know when a message has not been spoken by the LORD?" If what a prophet proclaims in the name of the LORD does not take place or come true, that is a message the LORD has not

> spoken. That prophet has spoken presumptuously. Do not be afraid of him" (Deuteronomy 18:21-22).

This verse teaches that Joseph Smith spoke presumptuously when he repeatedly claimed to speak *in the name of the Lord.* (See all the prophecies in *Doctrine & Covenants.*) Therefore, Mormons are not to fear him or heed his words for the simple reason his prophecies did not come to pass.

The following verses teach that even miracles are not necessarily proof of prophetic claims:

> If a prophet, or one who foretells by dreams, appears among you and announces to you a miraculous sign or wonder, and if the sign or wonder of which he has spoken takes place, and he says, "Let us follow other gods" (gods you have not known) "and let us worship them," you must not listen to the words of that prophet or dreamer. The LORD your God is testing you to find out whether you love him with all your heart and with all your soul. It is the LORD your God you must follow, and him you must revere. Keep his commands and obey him; serve him and hold fast to him. That prophet or dreamer must be put to death, because he preached rebellion against the LORD your God... (Deuteronomy 13:1-5).

Obviously, if a genuine miracle occurs but did not come from God, it had to come from the devil. And it is the devil that is most desirous of robbing God of His glory by having people worship false gods. Thus, the miraculous signs and visions of Joseph Smith are not to be heeded for the simple reason that he counseled people to follow and worship false gods rather than the God of the Bible. Thus, "*you must not listen to the words of that prophet.*" In effect, Smith preached rebellion against the Lord.

The following verses illustrate that those who follow their own visions and imaginations may be deceived into thinking they are receiving revelation from the Lord. In fact, they are so deceived they even expect their predictions to be fulfilled—but they are not fulfilled because God never spoke to such individuals in the first place:

> The word of the LORD came to me: "...Say to those who prophesy out of their own imagination: 'Hear the word of the LORD! This is what the Sovereign LORD says: Woe to the foolish prophets who follow their own spirit and have seen nothing!...Their visions are false and their divinations a lie. They say, "The LORD declares," when the LORD has not sent them; yet they expect their words to be fulfilled. Have you not seen false visions and uttered lying divinations when you say, "The LORD declares," though I have not spoken?' " (Ezekiel 13:1-7).

As a result of a false prophet's self-deceptions, God will be against him:

> Therefore this is what the Sovereign LORD says: Because of your false words and lying visions, I am against you, declares the Sovereign LORD. My hand will be against the prophets who see false visions and utter lying divinations. They will not belong to the council of my people... (Ezekiel 13:8-9).

Because false prophets lead people astray to worship false gods (and all that implies), God declares that He personally opposes those who see false visions and utter lying divinations. Mormons believe that Joseph Smith was a godly prophet and that God uniquely inspired Smith to reveal the original Christian gospel that the Christian church had corrupted. But the truth is far more sobering. Joseph Smith never repented of his gods or his beliefs. This means that God Himself was opposed to Joseph Smith. Clearly, false prophets are to have no place among the people of God. This should speak wisdom to those Christians who believe that Mormons are genuine Christians or who wish to stress commonalities with them for the sake of "Christian unity."

Almost everything mentioned in the following verses is applicable to Joseph Smith.

> Let no one be found among you...who practices divination or sorcery, interprets omens, engages in witchcraft, or casts spells, or who is a medium or spiritist or who consults

> the dead. Anyone who does these things is detestable to the LORD... (Deuteronomy 18:10-12).

Smith practiced divination and sorcery, aspects of witchcraft, interpreted omens, cast spells, was a spiritist, and consulted the dead. According to God, then, Joseph Smith was detestable to the Lord and could not have been His prophet.

Mormons should be challenged to study very carefully the practices and original prophecies of Joseph Smith to determine for themselves whether they are legitimate. Then, should they accept them, they alone will bear the responsibility.

What about the authority of the LDS church itself? As we documented in *Behind the Mask of Mormonism* and *What Do Mormons Really Believe?* modern Mormon church prophets have denied many of the teachings of the early Mormon prophets, such as Joseph Smith and Brigham Young. On what basis do they do this? Either these men were true prophets or they were not. If they were true prophets, then to change, deny, or suppress their revealed teachings is an act of rebellion and blasphemy against God. But if they were not true prophets, no one should have listened to them in the first place. In essence, because modern church authorities have ignored or altered their own prophets' teachings (teachings they shouldn't have listened to), they have no authority to command respect today.

Mormons should, in addition, be encouraged to independently investigate the truth claims of Christianity. If, as Socrates noted, the unexamined life is not worth living, this should also be true for the unexamined belief or religion.

If the most important thing in life is knowing and loving God—if God Himself declares we are to love Him with our entire mind (Matthew 22:37)—how are we really going to love God if we won't even examine the evidence to see if our faith is actually valid? We are not talking here about examining the "evidence" for Mormonism through the biased eyes of the Foundation for Ancient Research and Mormon Studies (FARMS) or the distorted apologetic research of BYU scholars (see Question 27). The real evidence needs to be examined objectively through the unprejudiced eyes of recognized history, logic, common sense, and, most importantly, the established doctrines of Christianity and biblical truth.

The weight of historical and other evidence against Mormonism is crushing, and this may explain why the majority of Mormons will not examine it. (Perhaps the best surveys to recommend are by former Mormons Jerald and Sandra Tanner, *The Changing World of Mormonism* [Moody Press], and the more scholarly text by Francis Beckwith, Carl Mosser, and Paul Owen, eds., *The New Mormon Challenge: Responding to the Latest Defenses of a Fast-Growing Movement.*) Mormons who are unwilling to read these books need to be encouraged to work through the reasons why. (Indeed, some of the most formidable literature proving that Mormonism cannot be a revelation from God can be found at the Tanners' Utah Lighthouse Ministry [PO Box 1884, Salt Lake City, UT, 84110]. They can be reached by phone at 801-485-8894 or at their website: www.utlm.org.) Also, there are many other quality resources available that supply specific techniques for reaching Mormons. These can be found through Alpha and Omega Ministries, Watchman Fellowship, and other organizations listed in the Authors' Note at the front of this book.

Another point is that if virtually everybody outside of Mormonism recognizes that it is not Christian, and yet Mormons have been told they are Christian, this alone should become an encouragement for members to examine the issue for themselves—independently from their church. Why is the Mormon view so disconnected from the rest of the world? Any church that can make such an incredible blunder should have the unexamined trust of no one.

Mormons might also be challenged to consider the practical consequences to themselves and their families for failing to prove the truth of their religion. The historic, prophetic, and scientific evidence for the truth of Christianity is compelling, as we documented in *Fast Facts on Defending Your Faith* (Harvest House,

2002) and other works. The evidence for Mormonism is nonexistent. For Mormonism to arrive 1800 years after the truths of Christianity are firmly established and claim to the whole world that Christianity is a damnable lie seems a bit presumptuous. Certainly, grand claims require grand evidence. For Mormonism to make these claims without offering a shred of evidence is pure bluff.

If Christianity is true, and the biblical Jesus Christ is the only way to God, then unrepentant faith in the Mormon Jesus will help no one. In fact, it will damn people forever. As Jesus said, "If you do not believe that I am [the one I claim to be], you will indeed die in your sins" (John 8:24). "I am the way and the truth and the life. No one comes to the Father except through me" (John 14:6). Based on the evidence for historic Christianity and the lack of evidence for Mormonism, LDS saints sit precipitously on the horns of a dilemma. If this simple fact—that the fate of their eternal soul hangs in the balance—is insufficient to gain their interest in a *truly* independent investigation of the issues surrounding the truth claims of Mormonism and Christianity, then probably nothing will.

Section VI
Miscellaneous Issues

24

What Is the Fruit of Mormonism?

No church is perfect, Christian or otherwise. The Mormon church, however, generally has a good, clean, positive reputation. Unfortunately, there is also another side to Mormonism. Often neglected, it is nevertheless required to give an accurate portrayal of the LDS faith. Mormons after all, can be expected to be like people everywhere, given the biblical portrait of man, both fallen and noble. But there are certain features of the LDS faith that weigh heavily against their image.

Jesus said that a bad tree was unable to produce good fruit. From a biblical and Christian perspective there is little argument that Mormonism is the product of a bad tree—that is, an occultist and false prophet named Joseph Smith instituted a new religion that was hostile to Christianity and rejected and opposed the one true God, His Word, and His Son.

Unfortunately, even the alleged good fruit in Mormonism—the LDS emphasis upon moral values, education, family, financial giving, helping the poor, and so on, has another side. Whatever good does exist we applaud. But these very benevolences also become the means for sustaining Mormonism and reproducing several hundred thousand new converts every year. So is Mormon fruit good, bad, or a mixture? When good things produce or lead to ultimately harmful consequences, the good things should not be endorsed uncritically as true fruit.

We are not trying to be unfriendly to Mormons, who are people we genuinely care about. There is a difference between criticism of a person and criticism of a person's religious beliefs. When religious beliefs are destructive to people's welfare, it is important—even necessary—to point out the errors and encourage biblical studies. At this juncture, we are merely explaining that appearances can be deceptive. Despite the good images of the LDS faith, the reality doesn't match the publicity.

So many people today conclude that Mormonism must be Christian due to all its "good fruit" that we feel a corrective is needed. Although we go into greater detail in our *Behind the Mask of Mormonism,* we'll touch on the main points here. Given the dramatic current and projected influence of Mormonism, and the fact that the Mormon church strongly emphasizes that it is to be known "by its fruits," we feel it's crucial to "test" the fruit to see if it's good all the way through.

On the surface, there are several aspects of Mormonism that seem to be above reproach. Mormon missionaries are extremely sacrificial in their willingness to give up two years of their lives to further their cause. That individual Mormons are committed to tithing shows a dedication to their church's standards and practices. The Mormons' emphasis on positive family values and the importance of placing the family first appears to be a wonderful role model. They also emphasize education at all levels and have a tremendous welfare program. However, all of these "positive" attributes lure unsuspecting individuals into a false religion that jeopardizes their eternal future. Another qualifier to these "fruits" is that they are reserved primarily for Mormons in good standing. The Mormon Church uses their social programs and family ties to entice and keep their members. A Mormon who leaves the church or questions church practices faces rejection by family members, divorce, loss of friends, and, sometimes, even his or her job. Consequently, there are many former Mormons struggling with social rejection, disillusionment, depression, divorce and other problems.[1] It should be evident that much or most of what is commonly considered "good" in Mormonism has a downside in keeping people from the true gospel and biblical Christianity.

In Matthew 7:15-20 Jesus taught,

> Beware of the false prophets, who come to you in sheep's clothing, but inwardly are ravenous wolves. You will know them by their fruits. Grapes are not gathered from thorn bushes nor figs from thistles, are they? So, every good tree bears good fruit, but the bad tree bears bad fruit. A good tree cannot produce bad fruit, nor can a bad tree produce good fruit. Every tree that does not bear good fruit is cut down and thrown into the fire. So then, you will know them by their fruits.

Jesus is speaking of false prophets here. The false prophets are disguised as innocent and gentle sheep. Despite their good appearance, "you will know them by their fruits." In other words, what they are in their nature, they will produce in their actions.

So, do Mormons have good fruit? On the surface, yes. But what must be considered the *principal* fruit of Mormonism? Is it not the nourishment, protection, and expansion of a false religion that undermines biblical truth in individual lives and society at large? Absolutely.

One indication of the troubles within Mormonism can be found in the fact that the Utah population is about 75 percent Mormon. Yet the social and economic problems in Utah are often worse than in other states. As of this writing, Utah has double the national average in bankruptcy[2] and one of the highest suicide rates.[3] Utah also apparently leads the nation in stock fraud and ranks above the national average in child abuse, teenage pregnancy, sexually transmitted diseases, and bigamy.[4] And in some ways, this may only be the tip of the iceberg.

We believe many of these problems stem from the *theology* of Mormonism itself—its false concept of God, which cannot logically justify absolute moral values, the strenuous emphasis upon works-salvation, self-perfection and so on. "Moral law must have a personal, eternal, transcendent, and perfect source. Such a being looks much like the God of classical Christianity and not much like the God of traditional Mormon thought."[5] The resultant guilt and frustration of self-perfection originates in the constant failure to live up to an unrealistic standard. Becoming a literal god through personal effort and good works can't possibly be an easy or accessible path.

The LDS church leadership itself has been guilty of unethical activities, which should have shaken the confidence of its members. LDS leaders have deliberately distorted the history and life of their own prophet, their own church history, historical facts, biblical teaching, and scripture itself.

If we look at early Mormon history, we find that many people were murdered because of the early LDS doctrine of blood atonement—that the death of Christ did not cover certain sins and the only way to be forgiven of those sins was to be executed. At least 11 crimes, most *not* capital crimes, were held by early Mormon leaders to be worthy of blood atonement (death). In 1876 former Mormon John Ahmanson wrote in his book *Secret History,* "Only the very smallest portion of the crimes of the Mormons have come to light, for who would recount them, after all? The dead do not talk, and murderers seldom are accustomed to bringing up the matter of their guilt. Even so, we shudder at the number of murderers that have been legally attested in Utah."[6]

Overt discrimination, polygamy, and occult practices disguised as religious rites are just some of the other questionable activities condoned by the Mormon Church for years.

Of course, the worst fruit of Mormonism is its betrayal of its own people in giving them a false god, a false savior, a false salvation, a false scripture, and a false hope of becoming gods in the afterlife—all of which will culminate in eternal separation from God.

Who can honestly study Mormon history and its fruit in the lives of its adherents and then claim that Mormonism is a good religion? All this is not to say that many individual Mormons are not good and decent people. They are. We bring these truths up to underscore the importance of not looking naively at Mormonism and accepting the public image of goodness. It's important to look below the surface to discover the truth about the fruit of Mormonism.

25

WHAT IS FARMS?

The Foundation for Ancient Research and Mormon Studies (FARMS) publishes literature in defense of Mormonism, especially the *Book of Mormon.* It describes its work in the following manner:

> The work of the Foundation rests on the premise that the Book of Mormon and other [LDS] scriptures were written by prophets of God. Belief in this premise—in the divinity of scripture—is a matter of faith. Religious truths require divine witness to establish the faith of the believer. While scholarly research cannot replace that witness, such studies may reinforce and encourage individual testimonies by fostering understanding and appreciation of the scriptures.[7]

FARMS has more than 100 Brigham Young University scholars working on its projects and a multimillion-dollar budget to pursue its goals: "They strongly believe that no other organization on earth can compete with their knowledge of the *Book of Mormon.* They are convinced that as far as human wisdom is concerned they are the ultimate experts on the subject. Consequently, they are very offended if anyone ignores or is ignorant of the research emanating from FARMS."[8]

Although this is clearly the most scholarly venue of Mormon apologetics, unfortunately for FARMS, its first ten years indicate the horse has stumbled at the gate. FARMS cannot defend what does not exist. Its literature may appear persuasive, but so does the literature of evolutionary scientists. Evolution seems persuasive to those wearing naturalistic spectacles because their assumptions cause them to ignore or misinterpret factual data they might otherwise accept. In a similar fashion, FARMS materials seem persuasive to those with Mormon spectacles because their assumptions cause them to ignore or misinterpret factual data they might otherwise accept.

Consider an illustration outside Mormonism. The *ABC Evening News* of June 2, 1998, reported upon a thorough investigation into the reason why the CIA so completely failed to ascertain that India was going to test nuclear bombs. It was not because the intelligence data was poor. The intelligence data was actually very clear—satellite images unmistakably showed the preparations underway for India's nuclear tests. The real problem was one of preexisting beliefs and, perhaps, naivete. The CIA was so convinced India would not explode a nuclear device that it was actually incapacitated from properly interpreting the evidence. The evidence was there, plainly in front of them. But it was not seen. As a result, the evidence that was there was missed or had to be interpreted otherwise. In a similar manner, Mormons may be so convinced of the truth of their religion that they become incapacitated when it comes to seeing and properly interpreting the evidence that is before them—in scripture and history—that discredits their beliefs.

When the basic arguments are examined critically in either case, whether of evolution or Mormonism, they simply do not stand. In fact, in neither case do they even have the possibility of standing. Naturalistic evolution was disproved the day Moses penned Genesis under divine inspiration. It was disproved on the basis of the authority of scripture and, as we documented in *Darwin's Leap of Faith* (Harvest House, 1998) and elsewhere, has always been disproved by the philosophical, common sense, and scientific data/arguments against it. In a similar fashion, Mormonism was disproved the day Joseph Smith wrote down and published his initial theology. It was disproved on the basis of the authority of scripture that proves it false and on the basis of the historical evidence against it. FARMS thus has an impossible job because it attempts an impossible task—successfully answering critics and "proving" Mormonism true.

Of course, FARMS does not directly claim to prove Mormonism, since the only real "proof" in Mormonism is the subjective "witness" of the "Holy Spirit" to the alleged divine origin of the *Book of Mormon* (Moroni 10:3-5). FARMS recognizes that it has little hard evidence, which probably explains why it spends so much time attacking critics of Mormonism and "correcting" their endless "errors." Nevertheless, in claiming to reinforce individual Mormon testimonies, and so forth, through scholarly means, it does suggest its work contributes to the evidential verification of Mormonism. Unfortunately, in making everyone's legitimate criticism and disproof of Mormonism look bad, rather than offering convincing evidence *for* Mormonism, it has established a track record that will be difficult to live down. As Dr. James White wrote in "Of Cities and Swords: The Impossible Task of Mormon Apologetics," "FARMS regularly promotes an image of scholarship, but serious problems with FARMS scholarship readily appear when they attempt to defend specific and unique elements of the claims of Mormonism....No veneer of scholarly acumen can make a culture appear in history that was not, in fact, there. And no amount of work by FARMS can make Joseph Smith something he was not: a prophet of God."[9]

Even Mormons have seen the problems with FARMS. For example, in "Why I No Longer Trust FARMS Review of Books" by John P. Hatch—an abstract (#215) given on August 10 at the 2001 Sunstone Symposium in Salt Lake City—Hatch stated:

> For the past twelve years, many Latter-day Saints have turned to the Foundation for Ancient Research and Mormon Studies (FARMS) and their semi-annual journal, FARMS Review of Books, as the unofficial response to anti-Mormon books and publications. I was one of them. However, when I began to dig beneath the surface of the blistering attacks in many of the FARMS reviews, I discovered

> many fallacies, inconsistencies, and even outright dishonesty. Once enamoured by FARMS and their unofficial mission to defend the faith, I am now aware of their often-unfair and brutal tactics, and I read the books for myself. This paper is an attempt to document and present many of the problems I have found in FARMS Review of Books.[10] (See Question 27 for more on FARMS.)

26

DO THE NEW LDS SCHOLARSHIP, EVANGELICAL RESPONSES, AND LDS/EVANGELICAL DIALOGUE NEED WORK?

For decades, by a variety of means, many responsible and self-sacrificing evangelical Christians have attempted to reach Mormons with the truth of the gospel. Two prominent examples that come to mind are former Mormons Jerald and Sandra Tanner (www.utlm.org) and Dr. James White of Alpha and Omega Ministries (www.aomin.org), but there are many others. We commend their sacrifice, dedication to truth, and quality research.

In recent years it has been claimed that Mormon scholars are now marshalling truly able defenses of Mormonism, that Mormons have answered most of the standard evangelical criticisms of their faith, and that the evangelical churches' response to Mormonism has become outdated or inadequate. Other evangelical scholars have implied or claimed that Mormonism may not be as opposed to Christianity as commonly thought.

As FARMS/BYU research and *The New Mormon Challenge* (2002) reveal, it is true that Mormon apologists/scholars have improved their learning and are attempting to more forcefully defend their faith academically.

Thankfully, the initial call to action by Drs. Mosser and Owens bore fruit from their hard labor and recent LDS scholarly apologetics are now being addressed, with several additional books in various stages of publication. While this new work is needed, it should be remembered that whatever work LDS scholars engage in cannot change established biblical, theological, and historic facts. Christian research has already, finally and decisively, disproved Mormonism's claim to be a new revelation from God on the basis of biblical doctrine, Christian apologetics, standard Mormon doctrine, and extensive historical research by Mormon, Christian, and secular researchers. While historical research is not infallible, it can reach a point where its conclusions are enormously likely.[11]

Mormon scholars will indeed continue to pour thousands of hours into making Mormonism seem like a true and credible faith, and thereby will confuse many. For this reason alone their arguments need to be addressed. But new research will not change conclusions already independently established. Consider the LDS scripture known as the Book of Abraham. Endless hours have been spent attempting to prove its legitimacy in light of critical attacks, but all in vain. "Latter-day Saint scholars with training in Egyptology have produced studies trying to give reasons to believe that the Book of Abraham is an ancient scriptural document, despite the universally acknowledged fact that its contents can by no means be described as a translation, in the usual sense of the word, of any of the extant Joseph Smith Papyri."[12] For example, *Apologia Report* for May 13, 2002 (gospelcom.net/apologia) reported that FARMS scholar John Gee "has argued that the extant portions of the Joseph Smith scroll in question [from which Smith falsely claimed to have translated the Book of Abraham] are incomplete, and that the original scroll included a large section—now missing—that may have contained the [actual] Book of Abraham."[13] In *Dialogue: A Journal of Mormon Thought* (Winter 2000), Robert K. Ritner, associate professor of Egyptology at the University of Chicago (who previously taught Egyptology at Yale, where he was John Gee's doctoral instructor) repudiates Gee's theory in "The 'Breathing Permit of Hor': Thirty-four Years Later." Here is "the first complete scholarly translation of three Joseph Smith Papyri (plus Facsimile 3, the original of which has not survived), widely understood to constitute the scroll the Mormon prophet identified as a lost record of the biblical patriarch Abraham and from which Smith claimed to translate the Book of Abraham (part of the LDS canon of scripture)." Ritner concludes that "...there is no reasonable expectation of any further text and certainly nothing even vaguely resembling the alien narrative of the 'Book of Abraham.'" "Of Gee's attempt to support Joseph Smith's misidentification of the Egyptian goddess Isis as 'King Pharaoh,' the god Osiris as 'Abraham, sitting upon Pharaoh's throne,' the female goddess Maat as 'Prince of Pharaoh,' and the black god Anubis as 'a slave,' Ritner writes: 'Such interpretations are uninspired fantasies and are defended only with the forfeiture of scholarly judgment and credibility.'" Edward H. Ashment, former Coordinator for Translation Services, Church of Jesus Christ of Latter-day Saints, and a doctoral candidate in Egyptology at the University of Chicago also disputes Gee's credibility in "The Use of Egyptian Magical Papyri to Authenticate the Book of Abraham."[14]

In essence, what we are looking at with newer LDS scholarship is a cleaning up after the plane crash. Long ago, Mormonism crashed irreparably on the mountains of scripture and history. No matter what the Church does, the plane is in too many pieces to put back together. An extraordinary effort might piece together a wing flap or even erect a part of the tail, but that's about it. So what can FARMS/LDS scholars do? Like die-hard evolutionists, they can muddy the waters with technical and seemingly convincing defenses of their faith—but they can never change facts.

Dr. Mosser argues that Mormons are now apparently attempting "to build the contextual superstructure necessary for a historico-grammatical interpretation" of the Bible, particularly the New Testament "that is both historically and culturally justified *and* at odds with orthodox Christian theology."[15] The Mormons are trying to lay the groundwork for an interpretation of the Bible that may *effectively* support Mormon beliefs. This is indeed a Herculean task and would mean the LDS church would have been able to undermine 2000 years of Christian scholarship. The flaws are already demonstrated in this Mormon approach because the facts of history and the accepted historical, grammatical interpretation of the New Testament establishes Christian doctrine, not Mormon doctrine. LDS efforts to establish their interpretive superstructure, at least for any objective analysis/interpretation of scripture, are fated to failure. Again, this does not mean such arguments should not be examined and refuted—they should be. But if LDS faith ever *is* capable of a robust defense scripturally and historically, then it is possible to put crashed airplanes back into the air as good as new. At that point Christianity itself becomes the myth.

Those most concerned about the new LDS scholarship do not find their latest evidence persuasive. "It should be obvious that we have read as much of this stuff as anyone, probably more than even most Mormons have, and we remain unconvinced. This ought to be a little troubling to the Latter-day saint who looks to FARMS for inspiration. We have read a good chunk of their best scholarship as charitably as we can and remain unpersuaded."[16]

Dr. Craig Hazen of Biola University is correct when he writes,

> In my opinion, the new Mormon apologists have a very long way to go to produce a convincing case for the truth of the Restoration through Joseph Smith Jr. I do not envy their task, because so many of the raw materials for a robust defense are missing. Mormon scholars have inherited a less-than-coherent metaphysic, a continued mistrust of the Bible, some difficult theological conundrums, and a devastating drought of "threshold" evidence that does not allow the broader scholarly community to take seriously the claims made in and about LDS sacred texts.[17]

Attempts at Dialogue

In 1992, we warned that there was an effort underway to reach or use evangelicals in order to make Mormonism seem evangelical, by emphasizing areas of "common ground." We have also seen this with Catholics in the "Evangelical and Catholics Together" statement (later emended), with Unification Church members in their Evangelical/Unification church dialogues, and others.

Not surprisingly, a number of books have recently been written by Mormons and evangelicals claiming that Mormonism and Christianity may not be so opposed as commonly believed. These include *How Wide the Divide? A Mormon and an Evangelical in Conversation*, by evangelical Christian scholar Dr. Craig Blomberg and Mormon scholar Dr. Stephen Robinson; Stephen Robinson's *Are Mormons Christian?* and *Believing Christ*; Richard R. Hopkin's *Biblical Mormonism*; as well as books on grace and justification by faith. LDS books such as these have added greatly to the confusion, despite failing to accomplish their goal of showing that the LDS faith is Christian.

In their book, Craig Blomberg of Denver Seminary and Stephen Robinson of Brigham Young University attempt a dialogue to show areas of agreement and difference. As I (Weldon) spent the first hour reading this book, I happened to hear in the background not one but two nationally televised ads of the Mormon Church attempting to draw in new converts. I thought it a bit ironic. Here I was reading a book by an evangelical Christian, a book that unfortunately confuses matters, while simultaneously thousands of people were responding to Mormon TV ads making them susceptible to a "gospel" that would place in jeopardy their souls. This is a point no dialogue will ever get beyond. Nevertheless, consider some of the claims and declarations of agreement (all page citations are from *How Wide the Divide?* 1997, InterVarsity). Dr. Robinson argues that, "Yes, Latter-day Saints believe things that Evangelicals do not, but the huge amount of doctrinal and scriptural overlap and agreement between us is much greater than the disagreement" (p. 60). Later, he declares, "As the Saints have returned to careful study of the Scriptures, we have been reminded of the importance of what we share with mainline Christians: Christ-centered living, the doctrine of the atonement, grace, justification by faith, and sanctification by the Spirit" (p. 67).

Dr. Blomberg and Dr. Robinson conclude together on the topic of Scripture that there was "more agreement between us than we had expected to find" (p. 75). Their joint conclusion on God is that "both Evangelicals and Latter-day Saints believe in an omniscient, omnipotent, omnipresent, infinite, eternal and unchangeable God" (pp. 109-110). Their joint conclusion on Christ and the Trinity is, "Both sides accept the biblical data about Christ and the Trinity, but interpret them by different extrabiblical standards (the ancient creeds for Evangelicals, the modern revelations of Joseph Smith for Mormons)" (p. 142). Their joint declaration on salvation concludes with the following: "Both Mormons and evangelicals trust that they will be brought into a right relationship with God by Jesus Christ, who is both the Son of God and God the Son. Both believed in the substitutionary atonement of Christ, justification by faith in Christ, and salvation by grace" (pp. 186-87). Later they emphasize, "In fact, adjusted for differences in terminology, the LDS doctrines of justification by faith and salvation by grace are not as different from Evangelical definitions as many on either side believe" (p. 193). Indeed, 12 "foundational propositions of the Christian gospel as we both understand it" are jointly affirmed (p. 195). And their conclusion on the atonement of Christ is that "we jointly affirm that his death on the cross completed an infinite, vicarious atonement that paid for the sins of the world and reconciled God and humanity" (p. 142).

Various reviews of this book show why evangelicals should be wary of trusting Mormons through such dialogues: The duplicity never seems to end. As Stephen F. Cannon points out in the *Quarterly Journal* (and as the Tanners have documented in numerous volumes), "If the LDS/MGS [magisterium] hadn't, through the years, engaged in publicly denying what has been privately believed and then trying to rewrite history to cover it all up, there wouldn't be the need to evaluate closely every word that proceeds from LDS church headquarters" (p. 30). (See Phil Roberts' review in the *Journal of Christian Apologetics*, Winter, 1997; or Cannon's review in the October–December 1997 *Quarterly Journal;* or the response by Mormon Dave Combe in "Truth-Telling and Shifting Theologies: An Analytical Look at *How Wide the Divide?*" from Salt Lake City *Sunstone*, Thursday, 7 August 1997, Session 166, 3:30–4:30 P.M.; or Dr. John White's review in the November–December 1997 *Christian Research Journal.*)

One wonders at the real outcome of such dialogue. The stated intent was to clarify; regrettably, it has confused many Mormons and Christians. Worse, uninformed churches and Christians who take the authors' advice at the end of the book may also leave themselves open to more than they bargained for: "Might we look forward to the day when youth groups or adult Sunday-school classes from Mormon and Evangelical churches in the same neighborhoods would gather periodically to share their beliefs with each other in love and for the sake of understanding, not proselytizing? (This has already happened in some places)" (p. 191).

If, as the authors concluded, "LDS doctrines of justification by faith and salvation by grace are not as different from Evangelical definitions as many on either side believe" (p. 193), how many young or uninformed Christians might just be open to accepting the Mormon church or even joining it? The Mormons are certainly not going to stop converting everyone they can to their faith. And it's a sure bet that the LDS church will take advantage of every opportunity presented to convert more Christians to Mormonism. That's part of their "new" agenda.

Not surprisingly, L. Ara Norwood, who writes reviews for FARMS, extolled "their landmark book" in his slanted review of Kurt Van Gorden's *Mormonism*, praising the authors for "demonstrat[ing] a mastery of openness and inquiry." To be frank, when someone as biased as Norwood (see the reference to Dr. White's response in Question 27) praises a book on Christian–Mormon dialogue, one can be certain that evangelical Christianity has not been the winner.

We think that evangelicals should reconsider this "new" approach to dialogue with Mormons. Dr. James White concluded as follows in his *Christian Research Journal* review of *How Wide the Divide?*:

> The most troubling issue raised by this book is not its inaccurate portrayal of Mormonism, nor even the confusion that that portrayal will inevitably cause many who read it. The most troubling issue is this: are we to be seeking this kind of dialogue?...Where, biblically, are we encouraged to lay out our areas of "agreement" with false teachers? Did Paul seek to minimize the gulf between himself and the false teachers in Galatia, or the gnostics in Colossae, by focusing on similarities?...The result is that the massive gulf that separates orthodox Christians and Mormons is in danger of being seen as a mere interpretational gap, rather than the canyon that yawns between those who worship the one eternal God and those who promote the exalted man-become-God of Joseph Smith (p. 31).

No doubt the motives are good in this kind of dialogue, but they always are. What is often not considered beforehand in endeavors of this type is the potential damage. The average Christian—not infrequently confused as to the true nature of Mormonism by lack of doctrinal study and fraudulent Mormon claims—is now further confirmed in his or her uncertainty or errors by well-meaning Christians who argue that Mormonism and Christianity are not so far apart as thought on key doctrinal points. The truth is that Mormonism is one of the most thoroughgoing anti-Christian religions in the world. And we do not use the term anti-Christian casually. Mormonism is not neutral toward Christianity; Mormonism actively opposes it. Because Mormonism is anti-Christian, to compromise with it can neither be considered a faithful defense of the gospel nor something conducive to the salvation of souls.

The Consequences of Confusion

To illustrate the confusion, some Christians are even calling some Mormons "evangelical Christians" and, as noted, many Mormons now claim to be "born-again" Christians. Given the projected growth rate and influence of Mormonism, this is hardly the time to confound theologies.

If a poll were conducted to determine how many Christians currently believe Mormons are Christian, we would not be surprised if the figure was embarrassingly high. Even former president and Southern Baptist Jimmy Carter illustrates our concerns at this point. According to *The Quarterly Journal:*

> [Carter has] denounced leaders of his denomination for declaring that professing members of The Church of Jesus Christ of Latter-day Saints are non-Christians....[The] former U.S. President also told the Mormon-owned *Deseret News* that his church's leaders were "narrow in their definition of what is a proper Christian or certainly even a proper Baptist." The newspaper also declared that Carter had misgivings about "Christians trying to convert other Christians" [Mormons].[18]

With confusion like this, Christians obviously need to be better informed on Mormonism—not to mention their own faith. We have always agreed with the sentiment expressed by Dr. Mosser in *The New Mormon Challenge:* "I'm convinced that a major factor contributing to Mormon growth is the widespread biblical and theological illiteracy among the laity of Protestant and Catholic churches. People in our churches need to be grounded better in basic biblical doctrine."[19]

27

HOW CREDIBLE IS LDS SCHOLARSHIP?

Scholarship is defined as a "standard of academic work" and "the systematized knowledge of a learned person, exhibiting accuracy, critical ability and thoroughness." Involved in the concepts of accuracy and critical ability, one assumes, is the power of judging rightly and then following the soundest conclusion allowable by an evaluation of the relevant data. Scholarship may not be officially defined as involving ethical considerations, but scholarship without ethics and objectivity is a blight upon learning.

While FARMS may have the appearance of scholarship, its agenda forces it to defend Mormonism at the cost of true scholarship. Any who doubt this need only read, for example, Dr. James White's website replies to reviews of his own scholarly material on Mormonism. (These include "A Study in FARMS Behavior," which is a review of L. Ara Norwood's review of White's *Letters to a Mormon Elder* [cf. White's reply to D.L. Barksdale's review of White's *Is the Mormon My Brother?*], and White's analysis of Drs. Peterson and Ricks' *Offenders for a Word* in *A Test Case of Scholarship.*)[20]

Significantly, even some Mormon scholars agree that Mormon scholarship in defense of Mormonism is generally untrustworthy. Karl C. Sandberg (DeWitt Wallace professor of French and Humanities, emeritus, Macalester College, St. Paul, MN), noted in "Whither (Mormon) Scholarship?" that there are Mormons who do scholarship in lots of areas, but not in Mormonism:

> There are Mormons who do scholarship in all the various disciplines—they play by the same rules as everyone else, they participate in the same dynamics, and they produce the same kind of knowledge. Such is not the case, however, when Mormons do scholarship about Mormonism or directly related subjects....Whenever a claim is raised that differs from the official view (the icon), the first duty, the immediate and only duty, is to defend the icon.[21]

Peterson and Ricks

An example of FARMS scholarship can be seen in Drs. Daniel C. Peterson and Stephen D. Ricks, *Offenders for a Word: How Anti-Mormons Play Word Games to Attack the Latter-day Saints* (Aspen 1992; FARMS 1998). Dr. Peterson is associate executive director and has been the chairman of the Board of Trustees for FARMS, and Dr. Ricks is a Board of Trustees member. Much of their book attempts to document the Mormon claim that the closer one gets to the (alleged) apostasy of the Christian church, the more that evidence for "original" Christianity—Mormonism—will be found. Peterson and Ricks cite the church fathers extensively. They allege, for example, that the early church fathers taught secret doctrines and rituals and believed in what is called the "deification" of man (theosis). They argue that this supports the Mormon doctrines of, respectively, secret temple ceremonies and exaltation—the doctrine that people can become gods. In their introduction they claim that their conclusions concerning early Christian materials "are fully justified by the evidence as well as by reason."[22]

But this is false. In the material that follows we will first supply a few of the comments of Dr. James White concerning Peterson and Ricks' claims about early Christianity, and then provide our own analysis in different areas. It is significant that Dr. White set aside the time to personally check their citations of the fathers by comparing them in the original context. As we will see, he shows how wrong Peterson and Ricks are and how often these Mormon scholars take quotations out of context to support their views.

First, "theosis" was a term used in a relative sense to explain man's creation in the image of God, giving him a spiritual nature, and that he could, by grace, attain union with God. Those who used the term never intended it to mean the Mormon doctrine of exaltation, or anything similar—that people could become gods and that the God of the Bible was once a man who progressed into Godhood by good works and righteous character. The church fathers would have been horrified by such ideas.

As to acceptance of alleged secret rituals in the fathers, Peterson and Ricks miscite, misinterpret, or fail to document their claims with Jeremias, Ignatius of Antioch, Tertullian, Origen, and others. For example, "Even a brief reading immediately communicates that Tertullian is, in fact, *arguing directly against the position attributed to him* by the misleading form of citation found in *Offenders*."[23] Dr. White then remarks, "All of us make mistakes. Sometimes we hurry, have deadlines, etc. One major error, such as the above, doesn't prove much. However, if a pattern of such misuse of sources can be discerned and documented, we have cause to wonder. *And just such a pattern can, indeed, be found.*"[24] After citing many additional examples of misquotation, Dr. White reflects,

> Any person desirous of honestly representing the beliefs of the early Fathers could not possibly ignore the context of the passages cited, yet, this is exactly what we find in Peterson and Ricks, and in the earlier work by [Stephen] Robinson [*Are Mormons Christian?* For a good critique, see the *Journal of Christian Apologetics,* Winter 1997]. Again we have to ask how this kind of a-contextual citation can end up in print, and, in fact, be reprinted by FARMS seven years later, without any correction or emendation, despite it having been pointed out in *Is the Mormon My Brother?* Scholarship means honestly dealing with historical facts, and quoting items fairly, and in context. How can these scholars present this kind of material? There are, however, many more examples of this kind of lack of concern for accurately handling the words of past Christian writers.[25]

With these preliminary comments aside, we now provide an additional scrutiny of *Offenders for a Word.* The extent of Drs. Peterson and Ricks' ignorance of Christianity and lack of sound scholarship can be seen in particular detail in the following citations and discussion. (All page numbers are cited from the 1998 FARMS edition):

> 1) "...the twenty-ninth chapter of the book of Isaiah... is...replete with prophecies of...the coming forth of the Book of Mormon" (p. xiii).

This is incredible, for the context of Isaiah 29 deals with the judgment of God upon Jerusalem (Ariel) for her wickedness. In vivid imagery we see that she is as ignorant of God's purposes as an illiterate man is of writing on a scroll. It does not and cannot, as LDS scholars have claimed, for example, refer to Mormon Martin Harris taking the *Book of Mormon* "gold plates" to a Professor Anthon who was unable to read them. We are unaware of a single biblical scholar anywhere in the world, outside the Mormon Church, who accepts Isaiah 29 as a legitimate prophecy of the *Book of Mormon.*

> 2)...examination discloses different views of Christ among the gospel writers, and the apparently older letters of Paul show "little interest in the supposed facts about Jesus" (p. 60, quoting C.L. Manschreck). As James D.G. Dunn points out, there was certainly "one Jesus" in history, but there have been "many Christs" in Christian belief—even (or especially) in the period of the New Testament (ibid.).

Peterson and Ricks' apparent confusion over who Christ is biblically cannot be used to blur the distinction between what is Christian and what is non-Christian. They believe that with so many different ideas about Jesus, "the question arises, just where on the opinion spectrum the line will be placed that separates 'Christian' from 'non-Christian'" (p. 61). They argue that one can hardly disqualify someone as a Christian (a follower of Christ) when we do not know exactly who Christ was. Obviously, they missed the point that if we don't know who Christ is biblically, then no one knows what a Christian is—not even Mormons, who can no longer be classified as Christians since no one now knows what a Christian really is.

But Peterson and Ricks are wrong. The gospel writers presented a consistent view of who Jesus Christ is. This means we can know with certainty that believing in this Jesus Christ makes one a Christian. Even Jesus said, "If you do not believe that I am [the one I claim to be], you will indeed die in your sins" (John 8:24). In fact, Jesus was so confident His teachings were clearly known that He appealed to His hearers even at His own trial: "I have spoken openly to the world....I said nothing in secret. Why question me? Ask those who heard me. Surely they know what I said" (John 18:20-21). Since Jesus identified who He was so clearly, we are surprised it could be lost on Drs. Peterson and Ricks.

In addition, there is no reason to think that the apostle Paul was suspicious of apostolic teaching about Christ, if this is their argument. For Paul to mention specific biographical details of Christ's life is unnecessary, unless it is relevant to his ministry. Indeed, he must have accepted the teachings of the gospel writers at this point because he never corrected or contradicted them, an impossible omission if he felt they were wrong, or if he disagreed with them over who Christ really was. Paul also taught that the apostles were the foundation of the church and that he himself was an apostle, proving not only his trust in their teachings, but his perceived unity with them (Ephesians 2:20).

> 3) Trinitarianism hardly seems a valid litmus test for determining who is, and who is not, Christian. Indeed, the metaphysical doctrine of the Trinity is a very late development, and hardly to be found with clarity in the Bible (p. 65).

If biblical accuracy on the nature of God is not a determiner of what it means to be Christian, nothing is. Are all nontrinitarians who claim to be Christian truly Christian? Peterson and Ricks are wrong again. The doctrine of the Trinity is clearly found in the Bible.[26]

> 4) If anyone claims to see in Jesus of Nazareth a personage of unique and preeminent authority, that individual should be considered Christian. Such is the consensus of both scholarly and everyday usage (p. 185).

Besides Mormons, this would make Jehovah's Witnesses Christian, as well as members of other non-Christian faiths.

> 5) A doctrine known as tritheism was taught by a number of prominent theologians in late antiquity, and can be considered "a definite phase in the history of Christian thought." It is never termed "non-Christian" (p. 67). Obviously, if ancient tritheists were Christians, there is no reason to deny that title to modern tritheists—even if we grant that term is an appropriate one to describe the Mormon understanding of the Godhead, which we do here only for the purposes of argument (p. 68).

This denial of Mormon tritheism (LDS believes in the Father, Son, and Holy Ghost as three separate gods) is sophistry. If Drs. Peterson and Ricks are unwilling to acknowledge Mormon tritheism, words lose all meaning. Tritheism is, of course, a form of polytheism, a belief in more than one god. This has never been Christian teaching because the Bible is clear that there is only one God (see Isaiah 44:6,8). The reason early Christians did not move toward tritheism as they grappled with the doctrine of the Trinity was because of the clear biblical emphasis on monotheism.

> 6) There are probably few communicant Mormons who would agree to being "polytheists," and none who would claim to worship more than one God....And the late elder Bruce R. McConkie's consistent instruction to worship the Father only and, in a certain sense, not even the Son, must surely be described as monotheistic (pp. 71-72).

Although McConkie denied LDS faith was polytheistic, he nevertheless wrote in his *Mormon Doctrine* (1977, p. 317), "There are three Gods—the Father, the Son and the Holy Ghost." Such belief in more than one God cannot logically be termed a monotheistic faith. Because Mormons believe in three gods for this earth and endless gods besides, Mormons are polytheists despite their consistent, if deceptive, denials. If we remember correctly, McConkie actually rejected worship of the Son (see section IV, note 14). To refuse worship to Jesus hardly makes one a Christian.

> 7) Mormonism teaches that human beings can become *like* God (p. 75, emphasis added).

In fact, Mormonism teaches that people become gods in the fullest sense, not just "like" God.

> 8)...being Arians in the first place did not banish the original followers of Arius from Christendom....Arianism is always termed Christian...as, generally, are the Unitarians (pp. 63-64).

One hardly knows how to respond to this. The church considered Arius and his followers heretics because the denial of cardinal

Christian beliefs by those within the church has always been considered heresy. Heresy involves the denial of vital revealed truth for the acceptance of serious error, and Arius was surely guilty of this in denying the Trinity. To deny such vital truths as the nature of God or the nature of salvation identified one as a deceiver, false teacher, and servant of the devil (Matthew 7:15-23; 2 Corinthians 11:2-4,13-15; Galatians 1:6-9; 2 Peter 2:1). This was grounds for separation or excommunication (Romans 16:17; 2 Corinthians 6:14-18; 2 John 10; cf. 2 Timothy 3:5,8; 1 John 2:19,26).

In the words of Robert M. Bowman, heresy in the strict sense is "a teaching or practice which compels true Christians to divide themselves from those who hold it."[27] Thus, the *Evangelical Dictionary of Theology* declares that Arius and all his followers were condemned, whether they were of the "moderate" wing that declared that Christ was of "like" (as opposed to the same) substance as the Father, or of the more radical wing that declared that He was not even of like substance as the Father. All were anathematized by the Council of Nicaea, which was convened on May 20, A.D. 325. Arius and all his followers argued that Christ was only a created being, not God the Son. This denied both Jesus and the Godhead. Thus the "council's anathemas were extended" to every aspect of Arianism—"to all those who claimed 'there was once when he was not'; 'before his generation he was not'; 'he was made out of nothing'; 'the Son of God was of another subsistence or substance'; and 'the Son of God [is] created or alterable or mutable.'"[28] Arianism had "reduced Christ to a demigod and, in effect, reintroduced polytheism into Christianity."[29]

While it is true many church leaders were swept into Arianism, this cannot change the fact that Arianism was anathematized or that Christians are specifically commanded to avoid false teachers (Romans 16:17). Harold O.J. Brown points out, concerning the gospel, in his important work *Heresies*,

> The early Christians felt a measure of tolerance for the pagans, even though they were persecuted by them, for the pagans were ignorant. "This ignorance," Paul told the

> Athenians, "God winked at" (Acts 17:30). But Paul did not wink at him who brought "any other Gospel" within the context of the Christian community. "Let him be accursed," he told the Galatian church (Galatians 1:8). Honorable enemies are regarded with less hostility than the traitor from within one's own camp. The Christian life is often presented as spiritual warfare. If the pagans are the enemies, the heretics are the traitors.[30]

Arians were heretics and traitors, despite the uninformed claims of Dr. Peterson and Dr. Ricks. Indeed, the issue of heresy is precisely the issue of Mormonism, for it denies, among others, the doctrine of salvation by grace, substituting salvation by works, and it denies the doctrine of the triune nature of God, substituting a theology of polytheism. Joseph Smith deliberately removed himself from the church when he rejected its teachings for his particular occult revelations (or inventions). The apostle John wrote, "They went out from us, but they did not really belong to us. For if they had belonged to us, they would have remained with us; but their going showed that none of them belonged to us" (1 John 2:19).

In order for Drs. Peterson and Ricks to make Mormonism Christian, the term "Christian" has to be redefined or made so mercurial that it can incorporate Mormon beliefs. As a result, the most fundamental misunderstandings of Christianity and biblical and historical theology arise, as can be seen in the following citations by the good doctors. The embarrassing thing is that Peterson and Ricks condemn themselves by redefining Christianity to incorporate Mormonism, even after stating the following:

> [There] exists a fairly coherent basic meaning to the term "Christian."...Since this meaning is well-established, latecomers have only a very limited ability to alter it....To use the word "Christian" in a new and different sense is to limit communication—or even mislead—until outsiders are able to decode and understand that new and different usage. We...shall argue that the historic meaning of the

> term is clearly broad enough to include The Church of Jesus Christ of Latter-day Saints... (p. 17).

Here is the "well-established" and "historic meaning" of "Christian" according to the *Oxford American Dictionary*, cited earlier. "Christian" is defined as "of the doctrines of Christianity, believing in or based on these." "Christianity" is defined as "the religion based on the belief that Christ was the incarnate Son of God and on his teachings." Mormonism clearly fails on both counts. Nevertheless, we'll summarize some of Peterson and Ricks' arguments.

1) *Biblical teaching does not disprove Mormon claims to be Christian.*

> Clearly, if it is thought to rest upon standards derived from the New Testament or from immediately postapostolic Christianity, the anti-Mormon case for expelling Mormons from Christendom is without substance (p. 41).

> ...the Bible offers no real reason to deny that Mormonism is Christian....[The] Bible cannot be used to define the Church of Jesus Christ of Latter-day Saints out of Christendom (pp. 43, 54).

> To repeat and stress the point: There seems, on the matter of scripture and canon, to be no reason whatever to deny that The Church of Jesus Christ of Latter-day Saints is Christian (p. 128).

The truth is that the Bible everywhere disproves the claim that Mormonism is Christian, as we have already documented in Questions 12-19.

2) *Even a false or heretical view of Jesus would still classify Mormons as Christians.*

> ...If the Mormons were partisans of an individual who... was in reality a wholly distinct individual from the Jesus of Nazareth whom mainstream Christians worship the world

> over, Latter-day Saint claims to be Christian could be dismissed *as true* but misleading (p. 55, emphasis added).

How could LDS claims to be Christian possibly still be true when they denied the central character of the Christian faith, Jesus Christ? Could Jesus have been clearer on this point? "He who rejects me rejects him who sent me" (Luke 10:16); "whoever rejects the Son will not see life, for God's wrath remains on him" (John 3:36). Thus, "no one who denies the Son has the Father" (1 John 2:23). Jesus Himself warned against accepting "false Christs" (Matthew 24:23-24), and the apostle Paul told the Corinthians that they were being deceived by Satan for accepting another Jesus (2 Corinthians 11:3-4).

3) *Points of similarity prove identity.*

This logical fallacy is seen where Peterson and Ricks offer 20 points of similarity between the Mormon Jesus and the Jesus of the Bible to show that they are the same person. "A comparison of twenty elements of personal identity possessed by 'the Mormon Jesus' and 'the Jesus of the Bible'—and many, many more elements could be compared...should make it clear to even the most hardened missing persons detective that the two are the same person" (pp. 57-58).

But Peterson and Ricks do not offer even *one* relevant comparison to prove identity of person! The points of similarity include things such as birthplace (Bethlehem), Jewish ethnicity, descent from King David, mother's name (Mary), occupation (carpenter), manner of death (crucifixion), time and place of death (under Pontius Pilate, outside Jerusalem), miracles, resurrection, ascension, and others. Even atheists, skeptics, and Buddhists would accept many of these, and numerous other cults would accept all these items. (Peterson and Ricks neglect to mention that in Alma 7:10, the *Book of Mormon* teaches Jesus was born in Jerusalem, not Bethlehem, so it can't be the same Jesus anyway.) Regardless, what is noticeably absent from their list is all those biblical teachings that would prove identity, like virgin-born, eternal Creator, eternally sinless, incarnate second person of the Trinity, and so on. And they understandably fail to mention all the specific teachings of Jesus which deny Mormonism, such as His belief in salvation by faith (John 5:24; 6:47) and in only one God (John 17:3).

4) *Mormon words and worldview have priority over biblical Christian words and worldview.*

> Do the Latter-day Saints somehow deny the Father and the Son? Not according to the first Article of Faith, which specifically affirms belief in both (p. 22).
>
> Do the Latter-day Saints deny that Jesus is the Son of God? No, for the first Article of Faith and literally hundreds of passages in their scriptural books teach his divine Sonship in the most explicit terms (p. 24).

Peterson and Ricks argue that merely mentioning the titles "Father" and "Son," or calling the Son divine, are sufficient to prove that Mormonism does not deny the Father and Son. They neglect to mention that Mormonism has an entirely different "Father" and "Son" than found in Christianity. Which religious cult doesn't mention the Father and Son?

5) *The New Testament meaning of the term "Christian" cannot be objectively determined.*

According to Peterson and Ricks, the applicability of the term "Christian" should be decided upon an individual's sincere claim to be Christian. Thus, because the New Testament allegedly gives no clear definition of what a Christian is, "by every New Testament standard, Mormons are Christians" (p. 31). Despite Mormonism having a different Christ, and despite Peterson and Ricks' uncertainty over who the biblical Christ was, "what made a person a Christian in the first century, and what makes a person a Christian today, is, simply, a commitment to Jesus Christ. Such commitment is central to the religion of the Latter-day Saints" (p. 27). "In point of fact, the Mormons are Christians precisely because they sincerely say they are" (p. 191). Well, we say, "Mormons *aren't* Christians precisely because we sincerely say they aren't."

So how are we to determine who is Christian and who is not? "It is not altogether clear that we have any responsibility, or any right, to make such a determination" (p. 184). We can, however, make such a determination by the New Testament standards that Peterson and Ricks ignore. We cite the dictionary definition again. The *Macmillan Dictionary for Students*: "one who believes in and follows the teachings of Jesus..." or "of the doctrines of Christianity, believing in or based on these." Such doctrines were derived from the New Testament and based on Jesus' teachings, which is why the apostle Paul emphasized, "You must teach what is in accord with sound doctrine" (Titus 2:1). It is why the apostle John warned, "Anyone who...does not continue in the teaching of Christ does not have God..." (2 John 9).

Drs. Peterson and Ricks, however, do make a determination about Christians who claim Mormonism isn't Christian. They cite Lloyd Averill's perception of "frustration, outrage, desperation, and latent violence" among Christians who oppose Mormonism (p. 180). They also refer to the "theological bloodlust" of much anti-Mormonism, which they say has a "supercharged, inquisitorial atmosphere" (p. 184).

Other Mormon Scholars

To give another illustration of the character of FARMS work, consider the text *New Approaches to the Book of Mormon* (Signature Books, 1993). This is authored by a group of Mormon and other scholars who are critical of the official Mormon story concerning Mormon origins, the *Book of Mormon*, and certain other Mormon beliefs. This book was reviewed by John Wm. Maddox in "A Listing of Points and Counterpoints" in *Review of Books on the Book of Mormon (RBBM)*, vol. 8, no. 1 (1996). In his review, Maddox attempts to show that the arguments allegedly refuting *New Approaches* published in RBBM's 566-page critique were legitimate criticisms. As he argues,

> Shortly after the *Review of Books on the Book of Mormon*, vol. 6, no. 1, was published, containing over 566 pages of responses to arguments raised in Brent L. Metcalfe's *New Approaches to the Book of Mormon* (Salt Lake City: Signature Books, 1993), a few people were heard to say that the FARMS publication had failed to address any substantive issues head on. That assessment did not seem to me to describe the contents of the *Review* that I had read. So I began going through both books to see how many substantive issues had been raised and addressed....I identified about 170 arguments raised in *New Approaches* that find responses in vol. 6, no. 1, or in subsequent issues of the *Review*....I found the responses of the reviewers to be cogent and sufficiently persuasive.[31]

But it all depends on what one finds convincing. Maddox may be convinced, but this does not change the fact that, clearly, FARMS has not dealt effectively with the material in *New Approaches.*

The following are verbatim illustrations we offer without comment. The term "Critics Claim" summarizes the initial criticism given in *New Approaches;* the term "FARMS Response" refers to the response by FARMS authors. Although some of the following material may be unfamiliar to those without a prior understanding of Mormon theology and history, the point we wish to make is that in every case, the FARMS response is either wrong or irrelevant. (Abbreviated documentary references have been deleted for ease of reading; also, the responses given often incorporate multiple authors.)

1. Critics Claim: The *Book of Mormon* reflects Trinitarianism.

FARMS Response: The *Book of Mormon* testifies of Jesus' Godhood. It does not fully explain the Godhead. Trinitarianism cannot be found in the *Book of Mormon* or the Bible.

2. Critics Claim: Sabellianism would explain Nephite belief in Jesus and the Father as two different manifestations of the same being.

FARMS Response: Sabellianism is only found by citing a few verses and ignoring the rest of the *Book of Mormon.*

3. *Critics Claim:* Comparing 3 Nephi and Matthew can help determine the historicity of the *Book of Mormon.*

FARMS Response: Nobody knows what was and was not in the original Greek.

4. *Critics Claim:* Eight mistranslations in the KJV are repeated in the *Book of Mormon.*

FARMS Response: The alleged mistranslations involve insubstantial differences. The differences are insignificant, especially in a nineteenth-century context.

5. *Critics Claim:* The *Book of Mormon* account of the sermon of Jesus is plagiarized from the KJV.

FARMS Response: This argument is neither proved nor disproved. Blind plagiarism cannot explain the complexity of the *Book of Mormon* account.

6. *Critics Claim:* The New Testament Jesus never claims to be the Father as in the *Book of Mormon.*

FARMS Response: The Old Testament and early Christian writers speak of Jesus as the Father.

7. *Critics Claim:* The cardinal directions in the *Book of Mormon* must be the same as ours.

FARMS Response: Directional concepts are accidents of culture and history.

8. *Critics Claim:* The traditional Latter-day Saint view is that all people in the *Book of Mormon* descended from Mulek or Lehi.

FARMS Response: The traditional view is not held officially by the Church.

9. *Critics Claim:* The traditional view is supported by the *Book of Mormon* text itself.

FARMS Response: This is not a careful reading of the text. Some passages from the *Book of Mormon* discredit this claim.

Some FARMS scholars themselves, despite their attempt to bolster Mormonism, have issued warnings about the tentative nature of their own research and all *Book of Mormon* research. This is commendable, but is this ever what Christians must do with standard apologetics? Do typical Christian apologetic works begin with the warning that the "chief source of evidence" for the truth of the Bible and Christianity is subjectively based, or that basic apologetic research is preliminary and conclusions may later be discarded? David Rolph Seely stated the following in his review of *Reexploring the Book of Mormon: The FARMS Updates* (Salt Lake City: Deseret Book and FARMS, 1992) in the *FARMS Review of Books on the Book of Mormon 5* (1993):

> The editor of this volume, John Welch, clearly delineates in his preface the intended purpose of the authors of the articles in this volume. Quoting from B.H. Roberts, he reminds us of the importance of the Holy Ghost as the "chief source of evidence for the truth of the Book of Mormon." And yet, following Roberts, "Secondary evidences in support of truth, like secondary causes in natural phenomena, may be of first-rate importance, and mighty factors in the achievement of God's purposes" (pp. xiii-xiv)....But it should be read with caution. Book of Mormon studies are still in their infancy. The editor and authors constantly remind us of the preliminary nature of most of these studies....There is still much to be done, much to be discussed, and many of these preliminary conclusions will be discarded, modified, and enlarged in the years to come.[32]

One might wonder about this, given the lack of academic freedom at BYU. Perhaps the quality of LDS scholarship is thus also hinted at by the June 13, 1998, vote of the delegates of the 84th annual meeting of the American Association of University Professors, which voted to censure Brigham Young University's administration, citing "infringements on academic freedom [that are] distressingly common at the university" and a "climate for academic freedom [that is] distressingly poor."[33] In other words, the Mormon Church tends to run academic matters for its own interests. In fact, the church response to the censure was simply to ignore it.[34]

In conclusion, FARMS may claim scholarship, but the truth lies elsewhere for precisely the reasons given earlier. The "defense" of myths and errors as genuine history is difficult to commend as a scholarly endeavor. If historical facts are absent, what is there to prove through scholarly analysis?

Dr. Hugh Nibley

No discussion of Mormon scholarship would be complete without considering Dr. Hugh Nibley, heralded by Mormons as the premier defender of the Mormon faith. Even evangelicals Mosser and Owen praise him highly:

> Hugh Nibley is without question the pioneer of LDS scholarship and apologetics....Since earning his Ph.D. at the University of California at Berkeley in 1939, Nibley has produced a seemingly endless stream of books and articles covering a dauntingly vast array of subject matter. Whether writing on Patristics, the Dead Sea Scrolls, the Apocrypha, the culture of the Ancient Near East or Mormonism, he demonstrates an impressive command of the original languages, primary texts and secondary literature. He has set a standard which younger LDS intellectuals are hard pressed to follow....The few evangelicals who are aware of Hugh Nibley often dismiss him as a fraud or pseudo-scholar. Those wanting to quickly dismiss his writings would do well to heed Madsen's warning: "Ill-wishing critics have suspected over the years that Nibley is wrenching his sources, hiding behind his footnotes, and reading into antique languages what no responsible scholar would ever read out. Unfortunately, few have the tools to do the checking." The bulk of Nibley's work has gone unchallenged by evangelicals despite the fact that he has been publishing relevant material since 1946....No doubt there are flaws in Nibley's work, but most counter-cultists do not

> have the tools to demonstrate this. Few have tried.... [Whatever] flaws may exist in his methodology, Nibley is a scholar of high caliber.[35]

As we mentioned earlier, a religion that has an inherently false theology must necessarily make numerous errors attempting to defend its beliefs doctrinally and historically. Certainly, this would also apply to the writings of Hugh Nibley, despite his scholarly status. Dr. James White's observation concerning FARMS scholars that "everybody cites Nibley, who, I am hardly alone in asserting, has never once cared about the contextual accuracy of anything he's ever cited" is to the point.[36] We have also found serious flaws in Nibley's assertions and documentation. This is not only because he is trying to defend the indefensible, but because when it comes to defending Mormonism, he sacrifices first-rate scholarship in favor of maintaining and propogating the belief that his religion, contrary to the solid research and evidence, is "Christian" and biblically sound. Here are two brief examples of detailed evangelical responses to Nibley's faulty scholarship.

> The Lachish Letters (Lachish ostraca) are late seventh-century B.C. documents that were found at Tell ed-Duweir (ancient Lachish) and written prior to the fall of the Southern kingdom of Judea. One of the reasons they are important is for dating the period, chronicling the fall of the last few cities of Judea. In *Book of Mormon Authorship: New Light on Ancient Origins,* edited by Noel B. Reynolds,[37] Dr. Nibley argues these letters have important parallels to the *Book of Mormon* (he lists 18 parallels), which allegedly illustrate the *Book of Mormon* as an ancient document. But the Lachish Letters cannot be used in this fashion. In "A Review of Hugh Nibley's Comparisons Between the Book of Mormon and the Lachish Letters,"[38] Dr. Thomas J. Finley, professor of Old Testament and Semitics at Talbot School of Theology in La Mirada, California, concluded: "All of the parallels given above are either invalid because of a lack of proper understanding of the Lachish Letters or because they can be explained more easily through parallels

> with the KJV. No good reason has been given to abandon the rather reasonable assumption that the *Book of Mormon* derives from the time of Joseph Smith and drew heavily on the King James Bible as a literary source."

Another example of Nibley's fundamentally flawed apologetics, again with detailed scholarly analysis, can be seen in Dr. James White's "The Gates of Hell" (www.aomin.org), where he critiques Nibley's biased interpretation of Matthew 16:18.[39] Dr. Nibley believes the gates of hell did overpower the Christian church. He believes the church was entirely apostatized and wasn't restored until Joseph Smith received his "divine" revelations in the nineteenth century. Here, Nibley argues that the "it" in "the gates of Hades will not overcome it" does not refer back to the church. From his perspective, it cannot refer to the church, so ways must be devised to reinterpret the obvious meaning of the passage:

> It must first be noted that Nibley's interpretation of the passage is not to be found in any stream of scholarly interpretation, whether Protestant or Catholic. We are not aware of a single scholar who attempts to say that the final phrase of Matthew 16:18 is referring to anything other than the Church; that is, that the "it" found in the phrase does not refer back to the term "church" mentioned immediately before. If Nibley is correct, it is amazing that exegetes over the centuries have missed what only he has discovered. Mormons are, by and large, in awe of Hugh Nibley's linguistic abilities. When Dr. Nibley says that the term "it" in Matthew 16:18 is "in the partitive genitive," that must be the case. Yet is it? [No, because, as White points out, there is no specific partitive genitive form in the Greek.] And what of all those translations of the Bible that do not catch this seemingly basic thing? No wonder Nibley replied to the critique of a Christian minister with, 'When ministers start making Greek the argument, it is time to adjourn."

It is also true that some Mormon scholars disagree quite strongly with Nibley's methodologies and conclusions. Their detailed responses and critiques are found at the "Honest Intellectual Inquiry" website.[40] (An example of a Mormon critique of Nibley's work is included in our note 40.) Careful scholars don't wrench sources, hide behind footnotes, and read into antique languages what is simply not there.

Here are a few examples from our own reading of Dr. Nibley, illustrating why we do not think he is a respectable scholar when it comes to adequately defending Mormonism or fairly evaluating Christianity.

In *Tinkling Cymbals*, Nibley cites Eduard Meyer's *Ursprung und Geschichte der Mormonen (Origin and History of the Mormons)* as illustrating "at length the 'exact identity' of his [Joseph Smith's] Church both in 'atmosphere' and sundry particulars with that of the early Christians. A 'striking and irrefutable' parallelism supports Mormon claims to revelation; 'with perfect right' they identify themselves with the apostolic church of old."[41] Since Meyer was "one of the best informed men who ever lived" and had "complete impartiality," according to Dr. Nibley,[42] he couldn't be wrong, could he? But the facts are that apostolic Christianity dovetails with Christian doctrine, not Mormon paganism, as 18 centuries of scholarship have proven.

Dr. Nibley claims solid, genuine evidence for his Church's most important scripture, the *Book of Mormon:* "Joseph Smith's own story of the book's authorship certainly lies far 'outside the usual and familiar,' and we have every right to ask for special proof of it."[43] "First and foremost, the Book of Mormon preaches the gospel, but it supports its presentation with strong evidence."[44] "Upon close examination all the many apparent contradictions in the Book of Mormon disappear. It passes the sure test of authenticity with flying colors."[45] And finally, "since it claims to be translated by divine power, the Book of Mormon also claims all the authority—and responsibility—of the original text."[46]

Yet speaking of his *Since Cumorah*, a defense of the *Book of Mormon*, "The whole thing may well impress some as disappointingly inconclusive, for we must insist that we have reached no final conclusions, even privately, and that all we can see ahead is more and ever more problems."[47] And "the evidence that will prove or disprove the Book of Mormon does not exist."[48] "By far the most important area in which the Book of Mormon is to be tested is in the reader's own heart. The challenge of Moroni 10:4 is by no means unscientific...."[49]

Which is it? "Special proof" or "disappointingly inconclusive" evidence? Do we endorse objective or subjective apologetics? Is the definition of science to include the physical or spiritual realm? Since *Book of Mormon* proof is entirely lacking, and disproof is abundant, Dr. Nibley, as a scholar, apparently has to sometimes make it seem like the book has real evidence when he knows better.

When it comes to the Bible and church history, things are not improved: "We are now assured that the three Synoptic Gospels are not the original Evangelion [gospel] at all....The very 'multiplicity of the Gospels' is adequate evidence that someone has been manipulating the records."[50] Dr. Nibley declares that early Christians "proceeded in the various churches to reinterpret and delete much of the record....[And] after the damage was done the New Testament went forth" throughout the world.[51]

The *Book of Mormon* verses Dr. Nibley discusses here are from 1 Nephi 13, which implies that Christ's gospel suffered great distortion at the hands of the early Christians. The *Book of Mormon* corrects the "devilish and abominable" distortions of the "great and abominable" Christian church by, for example, offering a gospel of salvation by works.[52]

But the apostle Paul unmistakably declares that the "gospel" of salvation by good works is under God's curse, so one has to question which church actually deserves the descriptions given. (See Galatians 1:6-9.) "We offer the Book of Mormon to the world in good faith, convinced that it is the truest of books."[53] "...Its one and only merit is truth. Without that merit, it is all that nonbelievers say it is."[54]

Regardless, "wherever we look in the ancient world the past has been controlled, but nowhere more rigorously than in the history of the Christian church. The methods of control, wherever we find them, fall under three general heads, which might be described as (a) the invention, (b) the destruction, and (c) the alteration of documents."[55] Again the facts are to the contrary. It is the history (and doctrine) of the LDS church that has been carefully controlled, as the Tanners' and others' research demonstrates repeatedly. Mormons are the ones who, unfortunately, have invented, destroyed, and altered documents in order to defend their interests.

These are only a few illustrations of why we don't trust the scholarship of Dr. Nibley. In the foreword to the 1952 edition of *Lehi in the Desert*, John A. Widtsoe remarked of Nibley's book, "It has been written also under the inspiration of the Spirit of God." With all due respect, we think not.

28

WHO DEFINES LDS FAITH?

> Among Latter-day Saints, his [Mormon president Gordon B. Hinkley's] interviews are also known for his ability to gloss over potentially unpopular church teachings to the point that some Saints have wondered, as President Hinkley admitted in a general conference, whether he in fact understands church doctrine.[56]

In *The New Mormon Challenge*, we read that

> ...one does well to distinguish between doctrinally binding Mormon theology, traditional Mormon theology, common Mormon beliefs, and that which is permissible as Mormon theology....The body of doctrinally binding LDS theology is surprisingly small. A fairly stable and large body of traditional LDS theology can easily be identified, but one soon realizes that Mormon theology is not static....The traditional LDS theology described in many books on Mormonism is, on many points, increasingly unrepresentative of what latter-day Saints actually believe.[57]

However, making such distinctions is not easy. The three editors and individual authors themselves have differing views on some matters: "In itself this lack of complete consensus testifies to the plurality of views and shifting currents one finds in contemporary Mormonism."[58]

So, how do we determine what "true" LDS faith is? If we look at the subject logically, it is difficult to identify a "true" faith as the overall historical theology is contradictory. If we assume the true faith is whatever the church happens to say it is at the present time, the problem is unresolved because it shifts with time and perceived church interest or needs. In either case, LDS faith becomes a relative faith that has little or no authority.

For example, the basic problem for FARMS research is that they insist on their own definition of what "Mormonism" is. Mormonism is bound by the standard works and what LDS authorities say it is, even though this *denies* official, earlier, divinely revealed church teachings. What is authoritative is only the *Book of Mormon, Doctrine & Covenants, Pearl of Great Price,* and the Bible—as interpreted by the General Authorities of the Church and the *current* apostles and prophets. While this involves quite a bit of material, it solves no problems because even here we find irreconcilable problems and contradictions.

Ezra Taft Benson's widely published, if incredible, 1980 speech at BYU, "Fourteen Fundamentals in Following the Prophets," threw out everything and argued that the *living* prophet is the only one to speak for the Lord in everything, is more important than the standard works and deceased prophets, will never lead the church astray, has no need for particular earthly training or credentials to speak or act on any subject, does not have to say "thus saith the Lord" to give scripture, and, happily, is not limited by man's reasoning capacities. At this point LDS faith becomes as mercurial as the shifting sands.

Thus, the General Authorities of the past are to be conveniently ignored at points of conflict or controversy, even though these men claimed to be apostles and prophets, and were accepted as apostles and prophets, and/or claimed divine revelation and inspiration. For example, President Hinckley, interviewed by Don Lattin of the *San Francisco Chronicle* (4/13/97), declared, "We have a great body of revelation, the vast majority of which came from the prophet Joseph Smith." Brigham Young claimed, "I have never yet preached a sermon and sent it out to the children of men, that they may not call scripture."[59] But the modern Church authorities, discarding "divine revelation" and vital history in the process, claim that only what *they* say is to be accepted. In essence, the church "guarantee of doctrinal accuracy" is restricted to current teachings only, with the undeclared recognition that its doctrines may change generation by generation, even perhaps president by president.

Unfortunately, it's not just that original and modern Mormonism are contradictory, it's that the Mormon scriptures themselves are contradictory, as noted earlier. For example, the *Book of Mormon* teaches both Sabellianism (the belief that the three persons of the Trinity are merely "modes," or "aspects" of the one God) and Trinitarianism, neither of which is "official" modern Mormon doctrine. As a divine revelation, this kind of contradiction makes Mormonism meaningless as far as determining any authoritative body of doctrine. When all is said and done, who or what is the Mormon god?

To illustrate the dilemma, consider the hypothetical parallel situation in evangelical Christianity and the implications. First, what would happen if the evangelical church declared as false doctrine numerous fundamental doctrines taught in the Old and New Testament by various prophets and apostles? Second, what if it claimed by divine decree that its modern teachings, ones that now contradicted earlier divinely inspired Scriptures, alone had final authority? Third, what if it ignored ethical standards to cover up resulting problems in order to help maintain the duplicity? If the evangelical church had done all this, evangelical Christianity would now be the modern fraud that Mormonism is—and it would deserve the exact same criticism and condemnation that Mormonism has received.

FARMS is free, of course, to complain about its Christian critics not understanding "true Mormonism," and to condemn them for engaging in careless scholarship. But until it deals seriously with its own religion, it can hardly be expected to be granted credibility in the eyes of those who know better. For its part, FARMS claims that it has no bias and is only interested in promoting the truth. The truth would seem to be closer to an interest in distorting or suppressing criticism. As Sandra Tanner noted,

> There can be no doubt that FARMS is intent on undermining the expanding influence of Signature Books [a publisher whose writers are critical of Mormonism]. In addition, FARMS wishes to destroy the work of Utah Lighthouse Ministry and that of other ministries working with Mormon people. Furthermore, as we will show below, they are willing to spend a great deal of money to accomplish their goals.[60]

At points, this becomes embarrassing. For example, in an alleged defense of Mormonism, FARMS and BYU scholars continue to cite the non-Mormon scholar Lawrence Foster's ill-fated attack on the Tanners. This is despite Foster's own belief concerning Mormonism that "the official line [of the Mormon story] is almost always wrong if you get down to the specifics."[61] He also accuses Mormon leadership of "bad religion" and of carrying its zeal to defend Mormonism at all costs to "pathological extremes."[62] He even agreed that in publishing all their works, "the Tanners probably care far more for the Mormon church [than] do the great majority of those Saints who have never rebelled or thought seriously about their faith...."[63]

This is a good point. It is not those Mormon scholars or authorities who distort facts and hide the truth who actually serve and care about Mormon people—it is Christians who have pointed out the truth about Mormonism. They do care about Mormon people. Telling people the truth is proof positive you do care for them. Hiding the truth from them is another story.

Mormon scholarship, real or imagined, can never change facts that have existed for over a century, no matter how sophisticated the argumentation. Has LDS scholarship successfully defended, rationalized or corroborated any of the following items?

- The serious confusion and contradiction between official Mormon doctrine historically and today.
- The enmity that Mormonism has shown toward the biblical God, Jesus, and Christianity throughout its history.
- The existence of a missing civilization.
- The crude, sexual polytheism and finite godism of Mormon theology.
- The nonstop Mormon defense of salvation by works, a doctrine the Bible declares is cursed of God.
- The Book of Abraham and other Mormon scriptures that contradict the Bible and, given Mormon claims for them, are proven fraudulent.
- That certain Mormon leaders, writers, and apologists should be trusted when they have a history of deception.
- That the fraudulent or occult "first vision" account of Joseph Smith condemning all Christian churches as an abomination to God was a revelation from the God of the Bible.
- That the occult activities of Joseph Smith and Mormonism, historically and in some cases today, are pleasing to God—that mediumism, astrology, divination, assisting or contacting the dead, and other occult practices can be blessed by God.
- That there was a complete apostasy of the Christian church, despite Jesus' promise that "the gates of hell will not prevail against [my church]."
- That Mormonism alone is the one true church on earth and Christianity an evil, apostate religion.

- That the Mormon priesthood of the unregenerate conveys the spiritual power and blessing of God.
- That Adam was the one true God, that created men and women can become gods, and that we have a "celestial mother" in heaven.
- That Jesus Christ should be belittled as merely one god among endless billions and be the product of a physical sex act between a male Mormon god and Mary.
- That the Christian church was evil and wrong in declaring justification by faith alone.
- That an eternal hell is not something the majority of humankind, if anyone, must concern himself or herself with.
- That Joseph Smith, despite his animosity toward Christianity, his occult practices, false prophecies, and the various evils in his personal life, was really a true and righteous prophet of God.
- That the errors, contradictions, and fabrications in Mormon scripture and authoritative LDS writings are academically defensible.

What is there for Mormon scholarship to defend here? Look also at the culpable things many Mormons have said about Christianity or Christians, or the harmful things some or many Mormons have done historically—opposed the gospel, hindered Christian missions, endorsed blood atonement, practiced deception, endorsed racism, defended the polygamy that infects Utah and other states even to this day, not to mention other evils masquerading as godly religion. If Mormonism were as devout and pristine an institution as proponents claim, how could Mormonism possibly be responsible for so many harms documented in numerous books—including the Tanners' works *Mormon Spies, Hughes and the CIA; The Mormon Purge; Unmasking a Mormon Spy;* in Mormon historian Dr. D. Michael Quinn's

Mormon Hierarchy: Extensions of Power; and in sociologist Anson Shupe's *The Darker Side of Virtue: Corruption, Scandal and the Mormon Empire?*

Sincere Mormon people who have been "taken in"[64] by Mormonism deserve better than this, and by God's grace they can and will discover the truth—if they will search for it. To be sure, Christians who believe that LDS faith is a biblical faith need to study even more diligently. As Paul said in 2 Corinthians 11:3-4,

> But I am afraid that just as Eve was deceived by the serpent's cunning, your minds may somehow be led astray from your sincere and pure devotion to Christ. For if someone comes to you and preaches a Jesus other than the Jesus we preached, or if you receive a different spirit from the one you received, or a different gospel from the one you accepted, you put up with it easily enough.

Other pertinent scriptures include:

> But even if we or an angel from heaven should preach a gospel other than the one we preached to you, let him be eternally condemned! (Galatians 1:8).

> For it is by grace you have been saved, through faith—and this not from yourselves, it is the gift of God—not by works, so that no one can boast (Ephesians 2:8-9).

> I tell you the truth, whoever hears my word and believes him who sent me has eternal life and will not be condemned; he has crossed over from death to life (John 5:24).

> For God so loved the world that he gave his one and only Son, that whoever believes in him shall not perish but have eternal life. For God did not send his Son into the world to condemn the world, but to save the world through him. Whoever believes in him is not condemned, but whoever does not believe stands condemned already because he has not believed in the name of God's one and only Son (John 3:16-18).

> And this is the testimony: God has given us eternal life, and this life is in his Son. He who has the Son has life; he who does not have the Son of God does not have life. I write these things to you who believe in the name of the Son of God so that you may know that you have eternal life (1 John 5:11-13).

DOCTRINAL SUMMARY

God: An exalted physical man; "Elohim" of the Old Testament; a deity "created" (technically, "fashioned") by the sexual union of his divine mother and father. As an infinite number of gods and earths exist, God the Father of Jesus Christ is creator and ruler of this earth only. He is (in early Mormonism) Adam who fell in the Garden of Eden, which was then located, according to Mormonism, in what is now Independence, Missouri.

Jesus: "Jehovah" of the Old Testament (Moroni 10:34 n.); the first begotten spirit child of Elohim ("God the Father"), who "created" (or "fashioned") Jesus by physical sexual union with Mary, one of his wives.

Trinity: Mormonism rejects the Christian Trinity for a belief in henotheism, the worship of one principal God (Elohim) among many. Mormonism is also tritheistic, stressing three primary earth gods, the Father, Son, and Holy Ghost, and it is polytheistic, accepting endless additional gods of other worlds.

Holy Ghost: A man with a spiritual body of matter.

Salvation: True salvation in Mormonism is achieved by personal merit and effort with the goal of attaining "exaltation," or godhood, in the highest part of the celestial kingdom. There, one may participate in "eternal increase"; that is, as a god one may beget (or fashion) innumerable spirit children just as Elohim has. All other salvation is considered "damnation," which to Mormons does include participation in various degrees of glory. Mormonism is almost universalistic, teaching that all will be saved except a very few "sons of perdition." Some Mormons teach that even these will be saved.

Death: Mormonism teaches that salvation is possible after physical death. Most people apparently go to a "waiting" area and are eventually assigned to one of three principal kingdoms where opportunities exist for advancement, possibly to a higher kingdom, at least according to some authorities.

Heaven and hell: There are three principal kingdoms of heaven. The celestial heaven is the highest, and below it are the terrestrial and telestial heavens. These constitute various "degrees of glory" and privilege. Personal entrance is based upon individual merit in this life, which is itself based upon individual merit in preexistence. In its most important sense, heaven consists only of three departments in the highest, or celestial, kingdom. Further, true salvation (exaltation, or godhood) is found only by those worthy to be granted access to the highest part of the celestial kingdom. Hell is not eternal, but a temporal purgatory. The vast majority who go there will, in their punishment, pay the penalty for their sins, be raised after the millennium, and inherit a "degree of glory." The only category of persons who apparently inherit literal eternal hell are "the sons of perdition," principally composed of a few apostate Mormons (Mormons who deny their faith) and possibly some adulterers or murderers.

Man: An eternal refashioned spirit intelligence having the innate capacity to evolve into godhood. Men on earth were first created as spirit offspring of Elohim and his wife through physical sexual intercourse. Thus, men are created or fashioned as preexistent spirits and subsequently inhabit the products of human sexual intercourse (a physical body) in order to attempt to gain exaltation or godhood.

The fall: Ultimately beneficial; predestined by Elohim for the spiritual progress and ultimate welfare of all mankind.

Sin: Mormonism holds a less than biblically orthodox view of sin in that its scriptural content is downplayed in some ways. First, the Mormon concept of works-salvation teaches that good works cancel the penalty of sin. Second, its teachings give the fall a positive role in fostering spiritual growth and maturity.

Satan and demons: Satan is one of the innumerable preexistent spirits created by Elohim and his wife; hence he is the spirit brother of all men and women, including Christ Himself. Because of his primeval rebellion, he was not permitted to inherit a body as were the rest of his brothers and sisters. In essence, Satan and demons once represented potential men and women but are now consigned to live as spirits forever.

The second coming of Christ: Mormons speak of the second coming of the earth god Jesus, but they have also referred to the second coming of the god Joseph Smith (*Journal of Discourses,* 7:289; 5:19).

The Bible: The Word of God as long as it is translated correctly. Wherever it disagrees with Mormon scripture or "official" theology, it is considered incorrect due to deliberate Christian textual corruption or false translation or interpretation.

Mormon "Articles of Faith"

1. We believe in God, the Eternal Father, and in His Son, Jesus Christ, and in the Holy Ghost.
2. We believe that men will be punished for their own sins, and not for Adam's transgression.
3. We believe that through the Atonement of Christ, all mankind may be saved, by obedience to the laws and ordinances of the Gospel.
4. We believe that the first principles and ordinances of the Gospel are: first, Faith in the Lord Jesus Christ; second, Repentance; third, Baptism by immersion for the remission of sins; fourth, Laying on of hands for the gift of the Holy Ghost.
5. We believe that a man must be called of God, by prophecy, and by the laying on of hands by those who are in authority, to preach the Gospel and administer in the ordinances thereof.
6. We believe in the same organization that existed in the Primitive Church, namely, apostles, prophets, pastors, teachers, evangelists, and so forth.
7. We believe in the gift of tongues, prophecy, revelation, visions, healing, interpretation of tongues, and so forth.
8. We believe the Bible to be the word of God as far as it is translated correctly; we also believe the Book of Mormon to be the word of God.
9. We believe all that God has revealed, all that He does now reveal, and we believe that He will yet reveal many great and important things pertaining to the Kingdom of God.
10. We believe in the literal gathering of Israel and in the restoration of the Ten Tribes; that Zion (the New Jerusalem) will be built upon this the American continent; that Christ will reign

personally upon the earth; and, that the earth will be renewed and receive its paradisiacal glory.

11. We claim the privilege of worshipping Almighty God according to the dictates of our own conscience, and allow all men the same privilege, let them worship how, where, or what they may.

12. We believe in being subject to kings, presidents, rulers, and magistrates, in obeying, honoring, and sustaining the law.

13. We believe in being honest, true, chaste, benevolent, virtuous, and in doing good to all men; indeed, we may say that we follow the admonition of Paul—We believe all things, we hope all things, we have endured many things, and hope to be able to endure all things. If there is anything virtuous, lovely, or of good report or praiseworthy, we seek after these things.[65]

Notes

Opening Quote

1. Gordon B. Hinckley, president of the Church of Jesus Christ of Latter-day Saints, quoted at official website www.mormon.org/question/faq/category/answer/0,9777,1601-1-55-2,00.html.

Section I: Introduction

1. See the National Council of Churches' 2002 *Yearbook of American and Canadian Churches*, Eileen Linder, ed. (Nashville: Abingdon Press, 2002).
2. Barna poll, "Religious Beliefs Vary Widely by Denomination," June 25, 2001, www.barna.org.
3. *The Salt Lake Tribune*, January 23, 1990.
4. See Joshua Decker, "Marketing Strategies of Mormonism" at www.saints alive.com/mormonism.
5. Francis J. Beckwith, Carl Mosser, and Paul Owen, eds., *The New Mormon Challenge* (Grand Rapids, MI: Zondervan, 2002), pp. 62-68.
6. Ibid., pp. 67-68.
7. John Ankerberg, "Mormonism Revisited" (Ed Decker with excerpts from the film *The God Makers)* (Chattanooga, TN: The John Ankerberg Show, 1983), television transcript.
8. *Time* magazine, July 29, 1991.
9. Richard N. and Joan K. Ostling, *Mormon America* (San Francisco: Harper, 2000), p. xvi, as quoted at www.irr.org/mit/Mormon=American=review.html.
10. *Time* magazine, July 29, 1991; *Denver Post*, November 21-28, 1982; *Wall Street Journal*, November 9, 1983; cf., *Arizona Republic*, June 30–July 3, 1991.
11. Walter Martin, *The Maze of Mormonism*, rev. ed. (Santa Ana, CA: Vison House Publishers, 1978), pp. 16-21.
12. In Ankerberg, "Mormonism Revisited," p. 22. See also John Heinerman and Anson Shupe, *The Mormon Corporate Empire* (Boston: Beacon Press, 1986).
13. According to the *New York Times*, August 1, 2002; *Wall Street Journal*, August 1, 2002.

14. Ankerberg, "Mormon Officials and Christian Scholars Compare Doctrine" *John Ankerberg Show*, television transcript, 1983, p. 21. See *Living a Christlike Life:* Discussion 5, pp. 14-15.
15. Martin, *Maze of Mormonism*, p. 21.
16. *The Utah Evangel*, Salt Lake City, UT, November 1981.
17. Martin, *Maze of Mormonism*, p. 20; Einar Anderson, *Inside Story of Mormonism* (Grand Rapids: MI: Kregel, 1974), p. ix; Jerald and Sandra Tanner, *Mormon Spies, Hughes and the CIA* (Salt Lake City: Utah Lighthouse Ministry, 1976), p. 56.
18. Martin, *Maze of Mormonism*, pp. 16-21.
19. *Christianity Today*, October 2, 1981, p. 70.
20. Ezra Taft Benson, *The Teachings of Ezra Taft Benson* (Salt Lake City: Bookcraft, 1988), p. 240.
21. Ibid., p. 238.
22. Ibid., p. 237.
23. *This People* (Mormon periodical), Spring 1990, p. 21. The 75-percent figure is from Josh McDowell and Don Stewart, *The Deceivers* (San Bernardino, CA: Here's Life Publishers, 1992), p. 16.
24. Ibid.
25. *Los Angeles Times*, January 6, 1990.
26. Bob Waldrep, "The Shifting Paradigms of Stephen Covey," at www.apologeticsindex.org.
27. Stephen Covey, *The Divine Center* (Salt Lake City: Bookcrafters Publishers, 1982), p. 240; see also Bill Gordon, "A Closer Look at Stephen Covey" at www.apologeticsindex.org.
28. Joseph Smith, *History of the Church* (Salt Lake City: Deseret Book Co., 1975), vol. I, 3. (*The Pearl of Great Price* excerpts are originally taken from this text.)
29. Ibid., pp. 4-6.
30. Ibid.
31. Ibid.
32. Ibid.
33. Ibid.
34. Ibid.
35. Ibid.
36. Ibid.
37. Ibid., p. 8.
38. Ibid., p. 9.
39. Ibid., pp. 11-12.
40. Ibid., pp. 12-14.
41. Ibid., p. 15.
42. For a summary of the documented changes and discrepancies, see Sandra Tanner, "Evolution of the First Vision and Teaching on God in Early Mormonism," at www.utlm.org.

Section II: *The Book of Mormon*

1. Joseph Smith as cited in Francis J. Beckwith, Carl Mosser, and Paul Owen, eds., *The New Mormon Challenge* (Grand Rapids, MI: Zondervan, 2002), p. 7.
2. Orson Pratt, *The Seer*, January 1853, pp. 15-16.
3. In the *Book of Mormon* Introduction—testimony of Joseph Smith—the Urim and Thummin are described as two stones in silver bows fastened to a breastplate. We do not know exactly what the Old Testament Urim and Thummim were. Nevertheless: 1) they were restricted in usage to the high priest; 2) the God of the Bible only rarely "spoke" through them to reveal His will; and 3) apparently they were two separate objects, not a single stone, which is what Smith used. Thus, in each category Mormon claims are refuted. Whatever Smith used, it was not the biblical Urim and Thummim (Exodus 28:30; Numbers 27:21). Joseph Smith was not an Old Testament high priest who used these implements to reveal God's will. He used an occult seer stone to divine the "translation" of a "text" that denies God's Word (cf. Mosiah 28 preface and verse 13).
4. David Whitmer, *An Address to All Believers in Christ by a Witness to the Divine Authenticity of the Book of Mormon* (Concord, CA: Pacific Publishing Co., 1887, reprint 1972), p. 12.
5. *The Saint's Herald,* May 19, 1888, p. 310.
6. See Jerald and Sandra Tanner, *Joseph Smith and Money Digging* (Salt Lake City: Utah Lighthouse Ministry, 1970), passim.
7. Joseph Fielding Smith, *Doctrines of Salvation* (Salt Lake City: Bookcraft, 1959), vol. 3, p. 225.
8. Einar Anderson, *Inside Story of Mormonism* (Grand Rapids, MI: Kregel, 1974), p. 61.
9. Fawn M. Brodie, *No Man Knows My History*, 2d ed. (New York: Alfred A. Knopf, 1976), pp. 69-70,72-73.
10. Hal Hougey, *A Parallel, The Basis of the Book of Mormon: B.H. Roberts' "Parallel" of the Book of Mormon to View of the Hebrews* (Concord, CA: Pacific Publishing, 1975), p. 4; Harry L. Ropp, *The Mormon Papers* (Downers Grove, IL: InterVarsity Press, 1987), retitled *Are the Mormon Scriptures Reliable?* p. 36.
11. Originally cited in *The Rocky Mountain Mason*, Billings, MT, January 1956, pp. 17-31; also in Jerald and Sandra Tanner, *Did Spaulding Write the Book of Mormon?* (Salt Lake City: Utah Lighthouse Ministry, 1977), p. 17.
12. Walter Martin, *The Maze of Mormonism,* rev. ed. (Santa Ana, CA: Vision House Publishers, 1978), p. 68.
13. Francis J. Beckwith, Carl Mosser, and Paul Owens, eds., *New Mormon Challenge* (Grand Rapids, MI: Zondervan, 2002), p. 366.
14. Ibid., p. 395.
15. Taken from the *Book of Mormon* and in part from McConkie, *Mormon Doctrine* (Salt Lake City: Bookcraft, 1977), pp. 528-29; Martin, *Maze*, pp. 47-49; Floyd McElveen, *Will the "Saints" Go Marching In?* (Glendale, CA: Regal, 1977), retitled *Mormon Illusion*, pp. 59-61; Gordon H. Fraser, *Is Mormonism Christian?* (Chicago: Moody Press, 1977), chapter 16; and Arthur Wallace, *Can Mormonism Be Proved Experimentally?* (Los Angeles: Arthur Wallace, 1973), chapter 9.

16. Martin, *Maze*, p. 328.
17. John Ankerberg and John Weldon, *Behind the Mask of Mormonism* (Eugene, OR: Harvest House, 1992), pp. 287-89.
18. *National Geographic*, letter of August 12, 1998 and Smithsonian letter of Sept. 28, 1997 to the Institute for Religious Research at http://www.irr.org/mit/natgeo.html.
19. Hal Hougey, *Archaeology and the Book of Mormon*, rev. ed. (Concord, CA: Pacific Publishing, 1970), pp. 3-4.
20. Raymond T. Matheny, lecture delivered at the 1984 Sunstone Theological Symposium in Salt Lake City. A typescript is located in Special Collections, Harold B. Lee Library, BrighamYoung University. See http://www.irr.org/mit/bomarch2.html; Michael Coe, "Mormons and Archaeology: An Outside View," *Dialogue: A Journal of Mormon Thought*, vol. 8, no. 2)
21. Norman L. Geisler and William E. Nix, *A General Introduction to the Bible*, rev. and exp. ed. (Chicago: Moody Press, 1986); F.F. Bruce, *The New Testament Documents: Are They Reliable?* (Downers Grove, IL: InterVarsity Press, 1971).
22. Ibid.
23. Cf., Jerald and Sandra Tanner, *The Changing World of Mormonism* (Chicago, Moody, 1981), pp. 369-70.
24. Robert K. Ritner, "The 'Breathing Permit of Hor': Thirty-four Years Later," *Dialogue: A Journal of Mormon Thought* (Winter 2000); Edward H. Ashment, "Joseph Smith's Identification of 'Abraham' in Papyrus JS1, the 'Breathing Permit of Hor'," *Dialogue: A Journal of Mormon Thought* (Winter 2000) and Ashment's 1993 work, "The Use of Egyptian Magical Papyri to Authenticate the Book of Abraham" at http://www.irr.org/mit/ashment1.html. Also see the compelling new documentary film, "The Lost Book of Abraham: Investigating a Remarkable Mormon Claim" (www.irr.org).
25. From Bob Witte, comp., *Where Does It Say That?* (Safety Harbor, FL: Ex-Mormons for Jesus Ministries, n.d.), p. 4.
26. Jerald and Sandra Tanner, *The Changing World of Mormonism* (Chicago: Moody Press, 1981), p. 560, citing *Improvement Era*, 16:344-345.
27. See the accounts in Ankerberg and Weldon, *Behind the Mask of Mormonism*, pp. 262, 273-74, 294-95, 299-300, 366-68.

Section III: Contradictions and False Prophecies in Mormon Scriptures

1. Church of Jesus Christ of Latter-day Saints, *A Sure Foundation*, p. 48.
2. Ezra Taft Benson, *The Teachings of Ezra Taft Benson* (Salt Lake City: Bookcraft Publishing, 1988), p. 116.
3. Hugh Nibley, "No Ma'am, That's Not History," p. 46, from Jerald and Sandra Tanner, *Mormonism—Shadow or Reality?* (Salt Lake City: Utah Lighthouse Ministry, 1974), p. 5.
4. John Ankerberg, "Mormon Officials and Christian Scholars Compare Doctrine," *John Ankerberg Show*, television transcript, 1983, p. 28.
5. John Ankerberg, "Mormonism Revisited" (Ed Decker with excerpts from the film *God Makers*), *John Ankerberg Show*, television transcript, 1983, p. 17.

6. Jerald and Sandra Tanner, *The Case Against Mormonism* (Salt Lake City: Utah Lighthouse Ministry, 1967-71), 1:86-87.
7. See Jerald and Sandra Tanner's website for more information: www.utlm.org/topicalindexc.htm#JSPolygamy; cf., Todd Compton, *In Sacred Loneliness: The Plural Wives of Joseph Smith* (Salt Lake City: Signature Books, 1997); see also the section on Smith at www.utlm.org/topicalindexc.htm#Smith,Joseph Jr.
8. See www.utlm.org/topical/indexb.htm#Suppression.
9. For another list see www.utlm.org/onlineresources/contra.htm.
10. Richard N. and Joan K. Ostling, *Mormon America* (San Francisco: Harper, 2000), pp. 382-83, as quoted at www. irr.org/mit/Mormon-America-review.html.
11. *The Evening and Morning Star,* July 1833, p. 1, emphasis added.
12. David Whitmer, *An Address to All Believers in Christ by a Witness to the Divine Authenticity of the Book of Mormon* (Concord, CA: Pacific Publishing Co., 1887, reprint 1972), pp. 30-31, emphasis added.
13. Ankerberg, "Mormon Officials," p. 7.
14. Joseph Smith, *History of the Church* (Salt Lake City: Deseret Book Co., 1975), 1:400.
15. Ibid., pp. 394, 400, 402; Walter Martin, *Maze of Mormonism,* rev. ed. (Santa Ana, CA: Vision House Publishers, 1978), pp. 353-54.
16. Smith, *History,* 5:336.
17. Cited in Jerald and Sandra Tanner, *Changing World,* p. 419, emphasis added.
18. Ibid., p. 420.
19. This was copied from the microfilm original at the Mormon Church Historian's Library; cf. Jerald and Sandra Tanner, *Changing World,* p. 420.
20. Ralson lists the following examples: *D&C,* 42:39; 62:6; 69:8; 84:114-115; 88:87; 97:19; 101:11,17; 103:6-7; 111:2,4-10; 112:15,19; 115:14,17; 117:12. Walter Martin refers to several false prophecies in *D&C,* 97:22-24 (with *D&C* commentary, appropriate section) and also in *Teachings of Joseph Smith* (pp. 17-18). Jerald and Sandra Tanner refer to false prophecies in *Journal of Discourses* 3:228,253, 262; 4:40; 5:10,93,94,164,173-74,274-75 and in other sources. The resource text, *Where Does It Say That?* by former Mormon Bob Witte, contains others.
21. Bob Witte, *Witnessing to Mormons, Using Where Does It Say That?* (Safety Harbor, FL: Ex-Mormons for Jesus Ministries, n.d.), p. 17.

Section IV: Mormonism and Christianity

1. Church of Jesus Christ of Latter-day Saints, *Doctrines of the Gospel,* p. 6.
2. Joseph Smith, *Teachings of the Prophet Joseph Smith* (Salt Lake City: Deseret Book Co., 1977), comp. Joseph Fielding Smith, p. 343.
3. James Talmage, *A Study of the Articles of Faith* (Salt Lake City: The Church of Jesus Christ of Latter-day Saints, 1974), p. 47.
4. Church of Jesus Christ of Latter-day Saints, *Sure Foundation,* p. 93.
5. Francis J. Beckwith, Carl Mosser, and Paul Owens, eds., *The New Mormon Challenge* (Grand Rapids, MI: Zondervan, 2002), p. 23.
6. Bruce McConkie, *Mormon Doctrine,* 2nd. ed. (Salt Lake City: Bookcraft, 1977), p. 579.

7. Robinson, *Are Mormons Christians?* (Salt Lake City: Bookcraft, 1991), p. 65.
8. *The Oxford American Dictionary* (Macmillan, 1984), s.v. "polytheism."
9. Church of Jesus Christ of Latter-day Saints, *Doctrines of the Gospel*, p. 16.
10. *Pearl of Great Price*, Book of Abraham 4:1; 5-11,14-17,25-29; 5:7-8,11,14.
11. McConkie, *Mormon Doctrine*, p. 317.
12. Church of Jesus Christ of Latter-day Saints, *Doctrines of the Gospel*, p. 6.
13. Ibid., p. 9.
14. McConkie, *Mormon Doctrine*, pp. 576-77.
15. *Journal of Discourses*, 7:333.
16. Robinson, *Are Mormons Christians?* p. 88, emphasis added.
17. Ibid., p. 79, emphasis added.
18. Ibid., p. 71, emphasis added.
19. Joseph Smith, *Teachings*, p. 372; cf., Joseph Fielding Smith, *Answers to Gospel Questions* (Salt Lake City: Deseret Book Co., 1966), 1:3.
20. Joseph Smith, *Teachings*, p. 370.
21. For an in-depth study of the historical development of the doctrine of the Trinity from apostolic times through the final form of the Nicean Creed adopted at the Council of Constantinople in A.D. 381, including a line-by-line comparison of the Creed with New Testament teaching, see Calvin Beisner's *God in Three Persons*. Two other excellent studies are E. Bickersteth's *The Trinity* and Robert Morey's *The Trinity*. E. Calvin Beisner, *God in Three Persons* (Wheaton, IL: Tyndale House, 1984); Edward Henry Bickersteth, *The Trinity* (Grand Rapids, MI: Kregel, 1969).
22. Smith, *Teachings*, pp. 347-48.
23. Church of Jesus Christ of Latter-day Saints, *Gospel Principles*, p. 293.
24. Joseph Smith, *History of the Church* (Salt Lake City: Deseret Book Co., 1975), 6:305.
25. Church of Jesus Christ of Latter-day Saints, *Gospel Principles*, p. 6.
26. Church of Jesus Christ of Latter-day Saints, *Doctrines of the Gospel*, p. 17.
27. Robinson, *Are Mormons Christians?* p. 60.
28. E.g., *Journal of Discourses*, 1:93,123; 6:120.
29. *Journal of Discourses*, 6:120.
30. *Journal of Discourses*, 11:286.
31. Joel B. Groat, review of Richard N. and Joan K. Ostling's *Mormon America*, for the Institute for Religious Research, www.irr.org/mit/Mormon-America-review.htm.
32. Gordon B. Hinckley with *San Francisco Chronicle* religion writer Don Lattin, with Richard Ostling in an interview for the PBS *NewsHour* with Jim Lehrer, and with *Time* magazine (August 4, 1997), www.irr.org/mit/Mormon-America-review.html.
33. Sterling M. McMurrin, *The Theological Foundations of the Mormon Religion* (Salt Lake City: University of Utah Press, 1977), p. 29.
34. Ibid., p. 36.

35. M. Russell Ballard, a member of the Quorum of the Twelve Apostles—official website www.mormon.org/question/faq/category/answer/0,9777,1601-1-1-56-2,00.html.
36. Gordon B. Hinckley, LDS president in Paris; *Deseret News,* June 20, 1998.
37. Church of Jesus Christ of Latter-day Saints, *What the Mormons Think of Christ,* 1982 (pamphlet), p. 16.
38. Church of Jesus Christ of Latter-day Saints, *Faith in the Lord Jesus Christ,* p. 4.
39. Robinson, *Are Mormons Christians?* p. 111.
40. McConkie, *Mormon Doctrine,* p. 169; cf., Joseph Fielding Smith, *Doctrines of Salvation* (Salt Lake City: Bookcraft, 1954-56), Bruce McConkie, comp., 1:75.
41. Church of Jesus Christ of Latter-day Saints, *Sure Foundation,* p. 224.
42. H. Evans, *An American Prophet,* 1933, p. 241, cited in Anthony Hoekema, *The Four Major Cults: Christian Science, Jehovah's Witnesses, Mormonism, Seventh-Day Adventism* (Grand Rapids, MI: William B. Eerdmans, 1970), p. 54.
43. McConkie, *Mormon Doctrine,* p. 129.
44. *Journal of Discourses,* 10:223.
45. See John Ankerberg and John Weldon, *What Do Mormons Really Believe?* (Eugene, OR: Harvest House Publishers, 2002), chapter 5.
46. *Journal of Discourses,* 1:50-51, emphasis added.
47. Joseph Fielding Smith, *Doctrines of Salvation,* 1:18, emphasis added.
48. McConkie, *Mormon Doctrine,* p. 547.
49. Benson, *Teachings,* pp. 6-7.
50. Hoekema, *Four Major Cults,* p. 56.
51. McConkie, *Mormon Doctrine,* p. 257.
52. Church of Jesus Christ of Latter-day Saints, *Doctrines of the Gospel,* p. 15.
53. Ibid., pp. 9-10.
54. Ezra Taft Benson, *The Teachings of Ezra Taft Benson* (Salt Lake City: Bookcraft Publishing, 1988), p. 6.
55. McConkie, *Doctrinal New Testament Commentary* (Salt Lake City: Bookcraft, 1976, 1977), 2:215.
56. Ibid., 3:238.
57. McConkie, *Mormon Doctrine,* p. 129.
58. Church of Jesus Christ of Latter-day Saints, *What the Mormons Think of Christ,* 1982 (pamphlet), p. 22; cf., McConkie, *Doctrinal New Testament Commentary,* 3:140.
59. Boyd K. Packer, acting president of the Quorum of the Twelve Apostles, BYU address, February 1, 1998.
60. McConkie, *Mormon Doctrine,* p. 670.
61. Church of Jesus Christ of Latter-day Saints, *What the Mormons Think,* p. 27.
62. Robinson, *Are Mormons Christians?* p. 109, emphasis added.
63. Einer Anderson, *Inside Story of Mormonism* (Grand Rapids, MI: Kregel, 1974), pp. 13, 19.
64. Talmage, *Articles of Faith,* p. 107.
65. Ibid., pp. 479-80.

66. McConkie, *Mormon Doctrine*, p. 671.
67. Joseph Fielding Smith, *Doctrines of Salvation*, 2:139.
68. LeGrand Richards, *A Marvelous Work and a Wonder* (Salt Lake City: Deseret Books, 1984), p. 25.
69. Orson Pratt, *Seer*, January 1854, pp. 199-200.
70. McConkie, *Mormon Doctrine*, p. 339.
71. McConkie, *Doctrinal New Testament Commentary*, 2:215; see also Richards, *Marvelous Work*, p. 275.
72. McConkie, Ibid., p. 229.
73. McConkie, *Doctrinal New Testament Commentary*, 2:238.
74. Ibid., p. 230.
75. Joseph Fielding Smith, *The Way to Perfection* (Salt Lake City: Genealogical Society of Utah), p. 189.
76. McConkie, *Doctrinal New Testament Commentary*, 3:402.
77. Richards, *Marvelous Work*, p. 275.
78. McConkie, *Doctrinal New Testament Commentary*, 2:248.
79. Spencer Kimball, *The Miracle of Forgiveness* (Salt Lake City: Bookcraft, 1989), p. 203.
80. Ibid., pp. 203-04.
81. Church of Jesus Christ of Latter-day Saints, *Doctrines of the Gospel*, pp. 49-50, emphasis added.
82. For an excellent popular study, see James I. Packer, *God's Words: Studies of Key Bible Themes* (Downers Grove, IL: InterVarsity, 1981).
83. Talmage, *Articles of Faith*, p. 76.
84. Church of Jesus Christ of Latter-day Saints, *Doctrines of the Gospel*, p. 22.
85. Talmage, *Articles of Faith*, p. 481; Joseph F. Smith, *Gospel Doctrine*, pp. 214-15.
86. Benson, *Teachings*, p. 14, emphasis added.
87. Ibid., p. 23.
88. Church of Jesus Christ of Latter-day Saints, *Sure Foundation*, p. 156, emphasis added.
89. Ankerberg, "Mormonism Revisited," p. 25.
90. Sterling M. McMurrin, *The Theological Foundations of the Mormon Religion* (Salt Lake City, 1965), p. 83.
91. For more information on this see John Ankerberg and John Weldon, *Astrology: Do the Heavens Rule Our Destiny?* (Eugene, OR: Harvest House Publishers, 1989), pp. 157-257.
92. D. Michael Quinn, *Early Mormonism and the Magic World View* (Salt Lake City: Signature Books, 1987), pp. 58, 60.
93. Ibid., pp. 78, 80.
94. Jerald and Sandra Tanner, *Changing World*, pp. 67-80.
95. *Discourses of Brigham Young*, pp. 378-380, citing *Journal of Discourses*, 7:332; 6:349.

96. Spencer W. Kimball, *The Miracle of Forgiveness* (Salt Lake City: Bookcraft Publishers, 1969), pp. 1, 5.
97. Ibid.
98. Duane S. Crowther, *Life Everlasting* (Salt Lake City: Bookcraft, 1988), p. 151.
99. Joseph F. Smith, *Gospel Doctrine*, pp. 436-37.
100. *Journal of Discourses*, 21:317-318, emphasis added.
101. Benson, *Teachings*, p. 35.
102. Walter Martin, *The Maze of Mormonism*, rev. ed. (Santa Ana, CA: Vision House Publishers, 1978), pp. 226-28, citing *Journal of Discourses*, 3:369.

Section V: A Critique of the LDS Claim to Be Christian

1. Daniel C. Peterson and Stephen D. Ricks, *Offenders for a Word* (Provo, UT: FARMS, 1998), p. 191.
2. Dr. Stephen Robinson, *Salt Lake Tribune*, January 12, 2002 in *Apologia Report*.
3. "Core Beliefs and Doctrines," www.lds.org/media2/library/display/0,6021,198-1-168-4,FF.html.
4. A more detailed critique in a variety of areas can be found in John Ankerberg and John Weldon, *Behind the Mask of Mormonism* (1996), *What Do Mormons Really Believe?* (2002), and at www.utlm.org.
5. *The Oxford American Dictionary*, s.v. "Christian."
6. Benson, *Teachings*, p. 10.
7. Church of Jesus Christ of Latter-day Saints, *A Sure Foundation*, p. 155.
8. John Ankerberg, "Mormonism Revisited" (Ed Decker with excerpts from the *God Makers*) (Chattanooga, TN: *John Ankerberg Show*, 1983, television transcript, p. 13.
9. While his book will undoubtedly convince many that Mormonism is a Christian religion, it will be convincing only to those who are unfamiliar with how to spot logical fallacies and lack knowledge of Mormon history and doctrine and biblical, historic, and systematic theology.
10. Stephen E. Robinson, *Are Mormons Christians?* p. vii.
11. Ibid., p. 2.
12. Ibid., p. 7.
13. See www.irr.org/mit/Stewart-analysis-of-Robinson.html.
14. Robinson, *Are Mormons Christians?* p. 34.
15. Ibid., pp. 72, 77.
16. Ibid., pp. 60, 88.
17. John Ankerberg, "Mormon Officials and Christian Scholars Compare Doctrine," *John Ankerberg Show*, 1983, Chattanooga, TN, television transcript, p. 32.
18. Text of 806-NonDis; found at www.gc2000.org/pets/cal/TEXT/c0806.asp.
19. Presbyterians and Latter-day Saints, Office of Ecumenical and Interfaith Relations at www.pcusa.org/pcusa/wmd/eir/mormon.htm.
20. See www.namb.net/evangelism/iev/Mormon/comparis.asp.
21. Per John Weldon's conversation with a representation of the WCC, March 26, 1999. Attempts to acquire an official statement were not responded to.

22. Sterling M. McMurrin, *The Theological Foundations of the Mormon Religion* (Salt Lake City, 1965), p. x.
23. Ibid., pp. ix, 26.
24. Fraser Gordon Holmes, *Is Mormonism Christian?* (Chicago: Moody, 1977), p. 10.
25. Martin, *Maze*, p. 45.
26. Jerald and Sandra Tanner, *The Changing World of Mormonism* (Chicago: Moody Press, 1981), p. 559.
27. Anthony Hoekema, *The Four Major Cults: Christian Science, Jehovah's Witnesses, Mormonism, Seventh-day Adventism* (Grand Rapids, MI: William B. Eerdmans, 1970), p. 30.
28. Irving Hexham, in Walter A. Elwell, ed., *Evangelical Dictionary of Theology* (Grand Rapids, MI: Baker Book House, 1984), p. 736.
29. *Encyclopedia Britannica*, 15th ed., Macropaedia, s.v. "Mormonism."
30. *The New Schaff-Herzog Encyclopedia of Religious Knowledge*, s.v. "Mormonism."
31. Anthony A. Hoekema, in J.D. Douglas, ed., *The New International Dictionary of the Christian Church*, rev. ed. (Grand Rapids, MI: Zondervan, 1979), p. 678.
32. See www.irr.org/mit/Stewart-analysis-of-Robinson.html.
33. Frances Beckwith, Carl Mosser, and Paul Owen, eds., *The New Mormon Challenge* (Grand Rapids, MI: Zondervan, 2002), p. 331.
34. John Ankerberg, "Mormon Officials and Christian Scholars Compare Doctrine" (1983), pp. 11, 14.
35. See www.lds.org/media2/library/display/0,6021,198-1-168-4,FF.html.
36. See www.utlm.org/onlinebooks/followingthebrethren.htm.
37. *Journal of Discourses*, 6:198.
38. Brigham Henry Roberts, "Introduction to Joseph Smith's History" in Joseph Smith, *History of the Church* (Salt Lake City: Deseret Book Co., 1975), p. lxxxvi.
39. Ibid.
40. *Elders' Journal*, 1, 4:59-60. This journal was edited by Joseph Smith. From Jerald and Sandra Tanner, *Mormonism—Shadow or Reality?* enlarged ed. (Salt Lake City: Utah Light Ministry, 1972), p. 3.
41. See *Book of Mormon* index references under "Babylon," "Church of the Devil," "Church, Great and Abominable," and "Churches, False" *Doctrine and Covenants* 29:21.
42. Joseph Smith, *Teachings of the Prophet Joseph Smith* (Salt Lake City: Deseret Book Co., 1977), comp. Joseph Fielding Smith, p. 270.
43. *Journal of Discourses*, 8:199.
44. Ibid., 8:171; cf. 7:333.
45. Ibid., 5:73.
46. Ibid., 5:229.
47. Ibid., 6:167.
48. Ibid., 5:240.
49. Ibid., 13:225.
50. Ibid., 6:25.

51. Pamphlets by Orson Pratt, p. 183; cited in Jerald and Sandra Tanner, *Case Against Mormonism* (Salt Lake City: Utah Lighthouse Ministry, 1967–71), 1903, reprint, 1:6.
52. B.H. Roberts, *The Mormon Doctrine of Deity: The Roberts–Van Donkt Discussion,* reprint (Bountiful, UT: Roberts/Horizon Publishers, n.d.), p. 233.
53. Pratt, *Seer,* May 1854, pp. 259-60.
54. Pratt, *Seer,* March 1854, pp. 237, 239-40.
55. Joseph Fielding Smith, *Doctrines of Salvation* (Salt Lake City: Bookcraft, 1976), Bruce McConkie, comp., 3:267, p. 287.
56. McConkie, *Mormon Doctrine* (Salt Lake City: Bookcraft, 1977), p. 132.
57. Ibid., pp. 137-38.
58. McConkie, *Doctrinal New Testament Commentary* (Salt Lake City: Bookcraft, 1976, 1977), 2:240, 274; cf., 3:265.
59. Ibid., 2:280.
60. Ibid., 3:85.
61. Ibid., pp. 247, 550-51.

Section VI: Miscellaneous Issues

1. See Orin Ryssman, "The Human Cost of Mormon Temple Marriage Policies," at www.irr.org/mit/temple-marriage-perspective.html.
2. *Deseret News,* Salt Lake City, UT, July 2, 2002.
3. Ibid., April 16, 2002.
4. See Utah Lighthouse Ministries at www.utml.org; *Deseret News,* Salt Lake City, UT, July 2, 2002 and August 11, 2002.
5. Francis J. Beckwith, Carl Mosser, and Paul Owen, eds., *The New Mormon Challenge* (Grand Rapids, MI: Zondervan, 2002), p. 240.
6. John Ahmanson, *Secret History: An Eyewitness Account of the Rise of Mormonism* (Chicago: Moody Press, 1984), Gleason L. Archer, trans., p. 391.
7. "About FARMS," at www.farmsresearch.com.
8. Jerald and Sandra Tanner, "Mormon FARMS: Battling the AntiMormonoids," Utah Lighthouse Ministry website printout, p. 8.
9. *Christian Research Journal,* Summer 1996, pp. 33, 35.
10. See http://www.sunstoneonline.com/symposium/frm-symp.asp?page-search. Session tape available-SL01215.
11. Will this always be so? I (John Weldon) have occasionally wondered whether or not the spirits that apparently gave Joseph Smith the LDS faith might have known something we don't. It is possible, however unlikely, that some kind of confirmation of *Book of Mormon* claims re: ancient civilizations could be forthcoming at some point. If so, would this change anything in terms of our basic attitude toward LDS faith? No, because no discoveries can ever bridge an unbridgeable gap between LDS theology and biblical teachings. Even if it were someday proved that the *Book of Mormon* were translated from an ancient text, its own content disproves it for qualification as a divine revelation.
12. Beckwith, et al., *The New Mormon Challenge,* 74.
13. See www.gospelcom.net/apologia.

14. See www.irr.org/mit/ashment1.html.
15. Carl Mosser and Paul Owen, "Mormon Scholarship, Apologetic and Evangelical Neglect: Losing the Battle and Not Knowing It?" *Trinity Journal,* Fall 1998. We used an earlier, widely circulated Internet copy that is essentially the same as the *Journal* article. This copy is online at www.apologeticsindex.org/cpoint10-2.html. It should be mentioned that Apologetics Index hosts articles for research and debate, without necessarily agreeing with the opinions expressed; Beckwith, et al., *The New Mormon Challenge,* p. 76.
16. Mosser and Owen, ibid.
17. Beckwith, et al., *The New Mormon Challenge,* p. 57.
18. *The Quarterly Journal,* vol. 18, no. 2, p. 3.
19. Beckwith, et al. *The New Mormon Challenge,* p. 69.
20. Alpha and Omega Ministries at www.aomin.org; Jerald and Sandra Tanner's three-volume response to FARMS, *Answering Mormon Scholars,* is also relevant.
21. *Sunstone,* December 1998, p. 10.
22. Daniel C. Peterson and Stephen D. Ricks, *Offenders for a Word: How Anti-Mormons Play Word Games to Attack the Latter-day Saints* (Aspen 1992; FARMS 1998), p. xiii.
23. James White, "A Test Case of Scholarship," unprinted paginated Internet copy, p. 14, emphasis added.
24. Ibid., p. 15, emphasis added.
25. Ibid., p. 17.
26. See Robert Morey's *The Trinity: Evidence and Issues* (Grand Rapids: Riverside World, 1996). The Athanasian Creed, which stresses the doctrine of the Trinity, says:

    > Whosoever will be saved, before all things it is necessary that he hold the catholic [universal] faith; Which faith except every one do keep whole and undefiled, without doubt he shall perish everlastingly.
    >
    > And the catholic [universal] faith is this: That we worship one God in Trinity, and Trinity in Unity; Neither confounding the persons nor dividing the substance. For there is one person of the Father, another of the Son, and another of the Holy Spirit.
    >
    > But the Godhead of the Father, of the Son, and of the Holy Spirit is all one, the glory equal, the majesty coeternal....
    >
    > This is the catholic [universal] faith, which except a man believe faithfully he cannot be saved.

27. Robert M. Bowman, "A Biblical Guide to Orthodoxy and Heresy—Part One: The Case for Doctrinal Discernment," *Christian Research Journal,* Summer 1990, Internet printout, p. 7.
28. V.L. Walter, "Arianism," in Walter A. Elwell, ed. *Evangelical Dictionary of Theology* (Grand Rapids, MI: Baker, 1984), pp. 74-75.
29. Ibid., p. 75.
30. Harold O.J. Brown, *Heresies* (Peabody, MA: Hendrickson Publishers, 1998), p. 3.

31. John Wm. Maddox. "A Listing of Points and Counterpoints," *Review of Books on the Book of Mormon,* vol. 8, no. 1 (1996), Internet.
32. Found at www.farmsresearch.com/review/5/Seely3. html.
33. Bryan Watterman, "Policing 'The Lord's University': The AAUP and BYU, 1995–1998," *Sunstone,* December 1998, p. 22.
34. Ibid., p. 36.
35. Mosser and Owen, "Mormon Scholarship, Apologetic and Evangelical Neglect," pp. 4-5.
36. James White, "A Study of FARMS Behavior," www.aomin.org.
37. FARMS Reprint Series, Provo, UT: FARMS, 1996, reprint of 1982 ed.; cf. Hugh Nibley, *The Prophetic Book of Mormon* (Salt Lake City: Deseret Book Co., 1989), ch. 18, "The Lachish Letters."
38. Thomas J. Finley, Institute for Religion Research, www.irr.org, a paper originally delivered to the Society for the Study of Alternative Religions (SSAR) at the annual meeting of the Evangelical Theological Society, November 19, 1998, Orlando, Florida.
39. James White, "The Gates of Hell," at www.aomin.org.
40. Honest Intellectual Inquiry, www.california.com/~rpcman/NIBLEY1.htm. We also found the following on the "Honest Intellectual Inquiry" website: www.california.com/~rpcman/NIBLEY1.htm. It discusses volume 1 of Nibley's collected works and seems to illustrate the quality of his works generally.

"For BYU Studies in 1988, Hugh Nibley received an unusual critique from Kent P. Jackson. I have heard others in the church express similar views, but to hear these things from someone like Jackson, published in something like BYU Studies, was a bit of a shock. It is refreshing to hear honest opinions like these from orthodox members. Portions of the article have been reproduced below....[These remarks refer to the *Collected Works of Hugh Nibley,* vol. 1, *Old Testament and Related Studies,* edited by John W. Welch, Gary P. Gillum, and Don E. Norton (Salt Lake City: Deseret Book Co. and the Foundation for Ancient Research and Mormon Studies, 1986), p. xiv.]

"Hugh Nibley is the best known and most highly revered of Latter-day Saint scholars....My own serious misgivings about his methodology do not detract from my admiration for his life of scholarship consecrated to the highest cause....Echoing the feelings of Nibley's followers throughout the Church, editor John W. Welch suggests in his Foreword that most of Nibley's lifetime total of nearly 200 titles are classics (ix). If that is in fact the case, then this volume has been severely shortchanged; nothing in it can be called a classic. It is, in fact, a disappointing collection.

"There are several areas about which I have concerns regarding the material in this book:

"1. In most of the articles Nibley shows a tendency to gather sources from a variety of cultures all over the ancient world, lump them all together, and then pick and choose the bits and pieces he wants....There are serious problems involved in this kind of methodology....Nibley creates an artificial synthesis that never, in reality, existed. The result would be unacceptable and no doubt unrecognizable to any of the original groups....

"This kind of method seems to work from the conclusions to the evidence—instead of the other way around. And too often it necessitates giving the sources an interpretation for which little support can be found elsewhere. I found myself time and time again disagreeing with this book's esoteric interpretations of Qumran passages. In several places Nibley sees things in the sources that simply don't seem to be there (for example, most of the preexistence references in the Dead Sea Scrolls, cited in chapter 7). This is what inevitably happens when scholars let their predetermined conclusions set the agenda for the evidence....

"2. In this book, Nibley often uses his secondary sources the same way he uses his primary sources—taking phrases out of context to establish points with which those whom he quotes would likely not agree. I asked myself frequently what some authors would think if they knew that someone was using their words the way Nibley does (the same question I asked myself concerning his ancient sources as well).

"3. Several of the articles lack sufficient documentation and some lack it altogether. This is to be expected in a collection that includes popular articles and transcripts of speeches. The editors clearly deserve our praise for trying to bring Nibley's footnotes up to professional standards. But given the complexity of the material, it was not always possible. The first article, for example, is riddled with undocumented quotations. Some of Nibley's most puzzling assertions remain undocumented—or unconvincingly documented—even in those articles that are footnoted heavily. The two most extensively referenced articles, "Treasures in the Heavens" and "Qumran and the Companions of the Cave," display the opposite problem. The seemingly endless footnotes in those articles suffer from dreary overkill, and yet too often I was disappointed by searching in vain in them for proof for the claims made in the text.

"4. Nibley frequently misrepresents his opponents' views (through overstatement, oversimplification, or removal from context) to the point that they are ludicrous, after which he has ample cause to criticize them. This may make amusing satire, but it is not scholarship....Among those satirized in this book are 'the learned' (8), archaeologists (chap. 2), 'the clergy' (38-39), 'professional scholars' (39), 'secular scholars' (39), 'the doctors' (217-18), 'the schoolmen' (217), and 'the doctors, ministers, and commentators' (221)....

"5. My final area of concern is more properly directed at the editors than at Hugh Nibley. What is the point of publishing some of this material?... Several of the chapters in this book, particularly 9 and 10, are so weak that the editors would have been doing Nibley a much greater honor if they had left them out. What is the point of resurrecting such material, which is now completely out-of-date and was not even quality work when first published three decades ago? In doing so they have not done Nibley a service, nor have they served his readers."

[The website piece continues]

"As noted in *BYU: A House of Faith*, by Bergera and Priddis, pg. 362 'As a former BYU history professor observed in 1984, "[Nibley] has been a security blanket for Latter-day Saints to whom dissonance is intolerable....His contribution to dissonance management is not so much what he has written, but that he has written. After knowing Hugh Nibley for forty years, I am of the opinion that he has been playing games with his readers all along.... Relatively few Latter-day Saints read the Nibley books that they give one another, or the copiously annotated articles that he has contributed to church publications. It is enough for most of us that they are there.'

"[And] reading Nibley reminds me of a quote from a line in Umberto Eco's 'Foucault's Pendulum,' which says, '...Wanting connections, we found connections—always, everywhere, and between everything.'"

At the same website, we found this: "I'm putting my own collection of Book of Mormon evidence together, and as I read this, it occurred to me that Nibley is horribly stretching the truth. In fact, I'd say he's lying....Because of everything else he incorrectly stated, I can't bring myself to believe that he's quoting the 1888 Enoch text accurately, or if he's translating it himself, manipulating the words to fit what he believes.

"Sorry, I'm Mormon, and I do respect Nibley's great efforts, but I draw the line at dishonest scholarship, which is what this appears to be."

41. Hugh Nibley, *Tinkling Cymbals and Sounding Brass* (Salt Lake City: Deseret Book Co. and FARMS, 1991), p. 11.
42. Ibid., p. 10.
43. Hugh Nibley, *The Prophetic Book of Mormon* (Salt Lake City: Deseret Book Co. and FARMS, 1989), p. 59, emphasis added.
44. Ibid., p. 498.
45. Ibid., p. 67, emphasis added.
46. Ibid., p. 69, emphasis added.
47. Hugh Nibley, *Since Cumorah* (Salt Lake City: Deseret Book Co. and FARMS, 1988), p. xiv, emphasis added.
48. Ibid.
49. Hugh Nibley, *An Approach to the Book of Mormon* (Salt Lake City: Deseret Book Co. and FARMS, 1988), p. 6, emphasis added.
50. Nibley, *Since Cumorah*, pp. 26-27.
51. Ibid., pp. 26-28.
52. We document this thoroughly in our *Behind the Mask of Mormonism* (Eugene, OR: Harvest House Publishers, 1992). See also Alma 7:16; Mosiah 5:8-9; 2 Nephi 9:23-24; 3 Nephi 27:14-17,21-22.
53. Nibley, *Approach*, p. 13.
54. Nibley, *Prophetic Book*, p. 86.
55. Hugh Nibley, *Mormonism and Early Christianity* (Salt Lake City: Deseret Book Co. and FARMS, 1987), p. 219.
56. "On the Record," *Sunstone: Mormon Experience Scholarship, Issues and Art*, December 1987, p. 70.

57. Beckwith, et al., *New Mormon Challenge*, p. 22.
58. Ibid.
59. *Journal of Discourses*, vol. 13, p. 95.
60. Jerald and Sandra Tanner, "Mormon FARMS: Battling the Anti-Mormonoids" (Salt Lake City: Utah Lighthouse Ministry), printout from www.utlm.org.
61. Ibid., p. 16.
62. Ibid., p. 25.
63. Ibid., p. 29
64. "Con" might be considered too strong a word, but in the case of LDS leadership, it seems appropriate as they know too much. We should emphasize that we do not believe individual Mormons necessarily deliberately con anyone; to the contrary, they are frequently kind and decent people. But they are often themselves victims, and because they are decent people, it makes the fact of the con all the more egregious. The LDS leadership has not only fleeced their own members, whom they claim to care for, by deliberately hiding the truth, but conned the public as well by claiming to represent biblical Christianity. Interestingly, if not amusingly, the word "con" has five meanings, positive or negative, all of which can be applied to Mormonism, including "against" (pro and con), "to examine or study carefully" (conning the page over and over), "to direct the steering of a vessel," "a person in jail" (a convict), and "to persuade or swindle after winning a person's confidence." Thus, despite the testimony of scripture and history as to true Christianity, Mormonism is clearly "con" (against) Christianity; therefore, members should take the time to 'con' (carefully study and examine) the LDS claims independently. And because LDS leadership and apologists have "conned" (steered) the ship of Mormonism in a particular direction, they have made "cons" of (spiritually imprisoned) the very people they claim to care for. Thus they are also "cons" in the unflattering sense: After winning peoples' confidence by various means, especially the holy act of prayer, they have proceeded to persuade them of the legitimacy of Mormonism, and thereby swindled them as to the truth.
65. See http://scriptures.lds.org/a_of_f/1.